Ocean City's beach scene, New Jersey

National Geographic's
Driving Guides to America

New York
And Pennsylvania
and New Jersey

By Randall Peffer
Photographed by Pete Souza

Prepared by
The Book Division
National Geographic Society
Washington, D.C.

Credits

**National Geographic's
Driving Guides To America
New York And Pennsylvania
and New Jersey**

By RANDALL PEFFER
Photographed by PETE SOUZA

Published by

THE NATIONAL GEOGRAPHIC SOCIETY

Reg Murphy
  President and Chief Executive Officer
Gilbert M. Grosvenor
  Chairman of the Board
Nina D. Hoffman
  Senior Vice President

Prepared by The Book Division

William R. Gray
  Vice President and Director
Charles Kogod
  Assistant Director
Barbara A. Payne
  Editorial Director

Driving Guides to America

Elizabeth L. Newhouse
  *Director of Travel Books
  and Series Editor*
Cinda Rose
  Art Director
Thomas B. Powell III
  Illustrations Editor
Caroline Hickey, Barbara A. Noe
  Senior Researchers
Carl Mehler
  Senior Map Editor and Designer

Staff for this book

Barbara A. Noe
  Editor
Margaret Bowen, Mary Luders
  Text Editors

Suez B. Kehl
  Designer
Thomas B. Powell III
  Illustrations Editor

Mark T. Fitzgerald
Sean M. Groom
Michael H. Higgins
Mary E. Jennings
Keith R. Moore
Justin A. Tejada
  Researchers

Tracey M. Wood
  Map Production Manager
Sven M. Dolling
  Map Researcher
Sven M. Dolling
  Map Production
Tibor G. Tóth
  Map Relief

Meredith C. Wilcox
  Illustrations Assistant
Richard S. Wain
  Production Project Manager
Lewis R. Bassford, Lyle Rosbotham
  Production

Kevin G. Craig, Mark T. Fitzgerald,
Dale M. Herring, Peggy J. Candore
  Staff Assistants

Susan Fels
  Indexer
Thomas B. Blabey
  Contributor

Manufacturing and Quality Management

George V. White, *Director*
John T. Dunn, *Associate Director*
Vincent P. Ryan, *Manager*

In Pennsylvania Dutch Country

Cover: New York City by night

Previous pages: Niagara Falls, New York
BOB CLEMENZ PHOTO

Facing page: Along the Atlantic City boardwalk, New Jersey

Library of Congress CIP data: page 160

4

Contents

6

Niagara Country ★

104

Niagara Falls 190

Buffalo

20

90

Lake Erie
and the
Alleghenies

219

5

Jamestown

17

Erie

17

79

6

6

219

OHIO

80

76

PENNSYLVANIA

220

30

Pittsburgh

Altoona

Laurel Highlands ★

30

70

99

76

30

79

219

220

70

WEST VIRGINIA

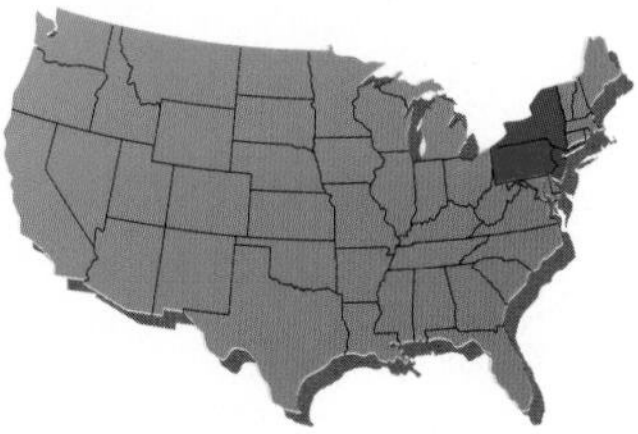

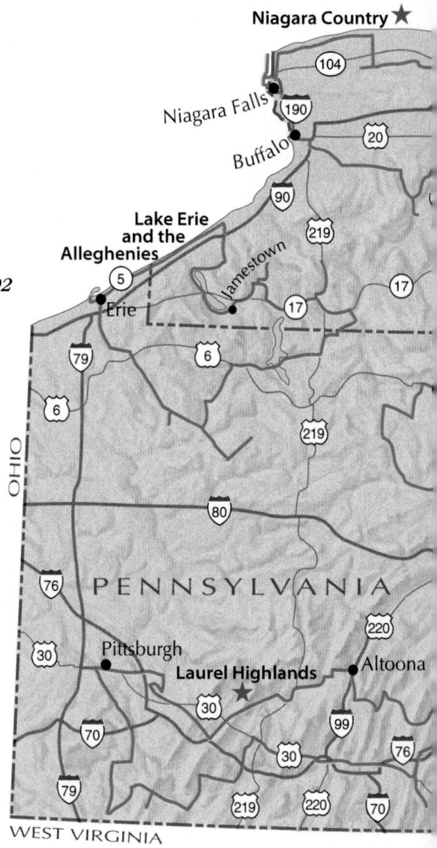

CANADA QUEBEC
U.S.

ONTARIO

87

37

30 3

**Thousand
Islands**

Adirondacks ★★

3
Watertown

30

22

81

NEW YORK

4

VERMONT

104

3

30

Rochester
90
Utica

Saratoga
Springs

Syracuse

20

87

Albany
20

**Finger
Lakes** ★

★
**Albany and
the Catskills**

90

MASS.

88

17
Elmira
Binghampton

17

220

81

6

★
**Hudson River
Valley**

CONN.

Poughkeepsie

**Bucktail
Wilderness**

Scranton

84

6

220
Williamsport

87

★ **Long Island
Idyll**

The Poconos
★

**The
Highlands**

80
Morristown

Museum Mile

Midtown ★★
495

Allentown

78
Newark

New York

The Neighborhoods

81

Lower Manhattan
★★

Harrisburg

**Pennsylvania
Dutch Country** ★★

**Philadelphia
Freedom Trail** ★★

95

Trenton

76

195

**Historic
Midlands**

31

83

30

Philadelphia
95

295

30

MARYLAND   DEL.

N.J. TPK.

NEW

JERSEY

Atlantic City

**Jersey Shore
Loop**

0   40 mi
0   60 km

*A*sk a New Yorker the key to enjoying life in the Big Apple, and you are bound to get a lot of answers. A sense of humor. A love of adventure. A tolerance for everything from English spoken with a dozen accents to the urban whir and chatter. One Park Avenue matriarch told me that the key to enjoying her city is a gold credit card…and winked. A youth sunning his tattoos and body piercings in Washington Square Park claimed that enjoying New York requires a passion for piña coladas and Chinese takeout.

But I think the keys to Gotham are feet. Sure, New York has its subways, buses, and cabs. But who enjoys them? To enjoy New York, you walk. To walk through a place is to know its soul.

Native people and European colonists also walked the

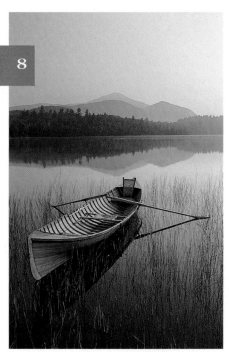

8

wild lands beyond the metropolis New Yorkers call "Upstate," "Jersey," and "Peeyay"—once the very fringe of the Eastern frontier. As a boy growing up in western Pennsylvania, I vacationed in the footsteps of those forebears who gave this area a history and culture. Such explorations, both by foot and wheel, have continued all my life.

In my native state I've discovered a character that goes far beyond the Ozlike glitter of Pittsburgh and the historic district in Philadelphia. The state is a wilderness ruled by its own "Grand Canyon," Appalachian Mountains, and hardwood forests. Its valleys harbor traditional communities of Amish and Quakers, Irish coalminers and railroaders.

It took me years to see that "Jersey" is more than a playground of sleepless Atlantic Cities and Victorian Cape Mays. In recent treks I've discovered the quiet beauty of the Delaware Bay and the million-acre forest called the Pine Barrens.

Connery Pond in the Adirondacks, New York

Upstate New York and the east end of Long Island are fraught with haunting edges—the brink of Niagara Falls, the summit of Whiteface Mountain, the jagged lakeshores, windswept Montauk Point.

So, when you pass this way traveling by wheel, imagine the mid-Atlantic as frontier. Think about walking the trails blazed by the Iroquois, Henry Hudson, and Harriet Tubman, for these lands will tell you a thousand stories.

RANDALL PEFFER

*N*ATIONAL GEOGRAPHIC'S DRIVING GUIDES TO AMERICA invite you on memorable road trips through the United States and Canada. Intended both as travel planners and companions, each volume guides you on preplanned tours over a wide variety of terrain to the best places to see and things to do. The authors, expert regional travel writers, star-rate (from none to two ★★) the drives and points of interest to make sure you don't miss their favorites.

In the stocks at Old Bedford Village, Pennsylvania

All distances and drive times are approximate (if you linger, as you should, plan on considerably more time). Recommended seasons are the best times to go, but roads and sites are open all year unless otherwise noted. Besides the stated days of operation, many sites close on national holidays. For the most up-to-date site information, it's best to call ahead when possible.

Then, with this book and a road map, set off on your adventure through this awesomely beautiful land.

9

MAP KEY and ABBREVIATIONS

National Historical Park .... N.H.P.	Featured Drive
National Military Park	
National Park	Interstate Highway
National Recreation Area	(95)
National Seashore	
Scenic and Recreational River	U.S. Federal Highway
	(1)
National Forest	State Road
Park	(14)
Plaza	
State Forest	Principal Canadian Highway
United Nations	(2)
Nature Preserve	County, Local, or Other Road
National Wildlife Refuge .... N.W.R.	[31]
State Park .... S.P.	Trail
Indian Reservation	State or National Border
City Center of Interest	Ferry
	FEATURED OTHER
	Tunnel

ADDITIONAL ABBREVIATIONS

Cr., CR. .... Creek
EXPY. .... Expressway
Ft. .... Fort
HIST. .... Historical
Mt.-s. .... Mount, Mountain-s
MUS. .... Museum
NAT. .... National
N.H.L. .... National Historic Landmark
NAT. MON. .... National Monument
N.H.S. .... National Historic Site
PKWY. .... Parkway
Pl. .... Place
S.H.S. .... State Historic Site
Sq. .... Square
TPK. .... Turnpike

Canal

State Forest Boundary

■ Point of Interest
★ State Capital   ═ Falls
+ Elevation, Peak | Dam

POPULATION

● **Philadelphia**   500,000 and over
● **Wilmington**   50,000 to under 500,000
● West Chester   under 50,000

Lower Manhattan★★

● **Walking tour** ● **2.5 miles** ● **1 day** ● **Year-round**

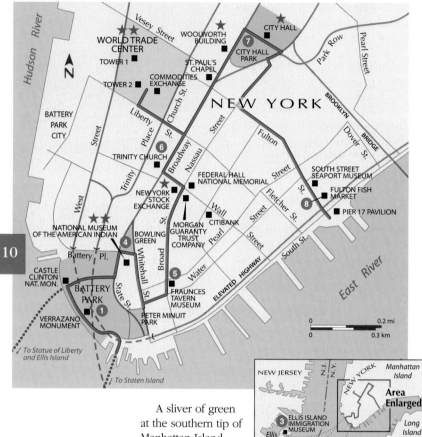

A sliver of green at the southern tip of Manhattan Island, Battery Park offers an unforgettable view of New York Harbor and the Statue of Liberty. It's fitting that New York should have such a sublime vantage point—particularly since this was the city's "front stoop" for millions of immigrants debarking from nearby Ellis Island.

Besides Battery Park's offerings, this walking tour explores rich architecture, historic sites, and a wonderful river setting. Starting from Battery Park, you board a ferry for a harbor view from the Staten Island Ferry, or one of the tour boats that ply to the Statue of Liberty and the Ellis Island Museum of Immigration. When you return to shore, you visit sites highlighting the city's heritage, which dates back to 1626, when Dutchman Peter Minuit bought Manhattan from Indians for $24 worth of baubles. Moving northwest along Wall Street, you immerse yourself in the hustle of the world's foremost financial district, with the twin peaks of the World Trade Center and the "Cathedral of Commerce," the Woolworth Building, towering above. But you will find an escape from the crowd of "white shirts" (financial traders), on the grounds of Trinity Church, City Hall Park, and the piers of South Street Seaport, where tall ships reign.

Thank the Dutch for the starting point on this walk, ❶ **Battery Park.** This green apron on Manhattan's point constitutes a landfill that began shortly after Dutch colonists arrived in 1626 and started developing the terrain. Over the years, construction debris has added several acres to the island's tip, completely filling in the 200 feet between the shore and the park's focal point, **Castle Clinton National Monument** *(212-344-7220)*. Completed in 1811, the harbor fortification with 8-foot walls and 28 cannons never fired a shot in anger. Through the years it has had long careers as an entertainment venue—where the great Jenny Lind sang—and the New York Aquarium. But the Castle's greatest contribution to American history lies in its role as an immigration landing depot from 1855 to 1890. Nearly eight million immigrants, two out of three new arrivals in America during those years, entered through the Castle. Today, the fort contains a museum documenting its history; it's also the place where you buy boat-ride tickets to the Statue of Liberty and Ellis Island.

Before you take to the water, the park is well worth a stroll, particularly on an early summer morning. Get some coffee from a vendor, enjoy the sea breeze, the shade trees, and the fanciful **Verrazano Monument,** recognizing the unheralded Italian discovery of the island in 1524. Notice the presence of police and sanitation workers sprucing up the park—signs that New York is committed to being a cleaner, safer place than it was just a few years ago.

When you feel the urge "to get to sea," as Herman Melville did while water gazing from the Battery, your choice of routes depends on time and money. The **Staten Island Ferry** *(S end of Battery Park. 718-815-BOAT)* remains the cheapest harbor tour in the world—free. The best sightseeing comes when you board one of the older, open-decked ferries. Feel the wind and get an

Statue of Liberty

11

Ellis Island Immigration Museum with Lower Manhattan backdrop

unobstructed view of Miss Liberty and Ellis Island as you sail past. The round-trip takes less than an hour. You may want to bring some fresh bagels or fruit salad aboard for a light breakfast al fresco.

The **Circle Line-Statue of Liberty Ferry** *(Battery Park. 212-269-5755. Fare)* makes a loop, stopping first at Liberty, then Ellis Island, so you can get off and return at will. The only snag is the crowd; there are lines for these boats almost everyday. And once you get to the ❷ **Statue of Liberty National Monument** *(212-363-3200),* the wait to climb to her crown can take hours. If you arrive after 2 p.m., you might even be turned away. For those who don't make it to the top, there is a museum and video in the pedestal to salve the disappointment.

But you don't have to climb to the crown to appreciate Liberty: Many visitors find that just stopping at her feet is an inspiring pilgrimage. The statue was a gift from France; she was shipped to the U.S., assembled, and formally dedicated in 1886. Sculptor Frédéric-Auguste Bartholdi made her 50 feet taller than the Colossus of Rhodes. She rises 151 feet above her 10-story pedestal, and her copper sheathing weighs over 220 tons.

❸ **Ellis Island Immigration Museum** *(212-363-3200)* makes the perfect sequel to Liberty. Between 1892 and 1954, more than 12 million immigrants landed here for medical and legal processing. Today, one of three Americans can trace an ancestor or relative to the Ellis Island center. After years of abandonment, it reopened in 1990 as part of the Statue of Liberty National Monument. Legions have come ever since to follow in their ancestors' footsteps. Visit the Baggage Room, Registry Room, Great Hall, and more than 30 galleries of artifacts, photos, oral

At the National Museum of the American Indian

histories, and ethnic music. You can also view a powerful documentary. The Wall of Honor overlooking the Statue of Liberty includes the names of over 400,000 immigrants. The island's green spaces make fine picnic sites.

Returning to Manhattan, head up State Street to the foot of Broadway and the ❹ **Bowling Green.** The city's oldest existing park, it dates from 1734. During colonial times a statue of King George III stood here, but patriots tumbled the statue after listening to a reading of the Declaration of Independence in July 1776, and melted it to make bullets. Today, the green makes a vantage point from which to view the **Alexander Hamilton Customs House** *(1 Bowling Green).* This is one of the finest beaux arts buildings in New York City. The facade's four sculptures representing Asia, Europe, Africa, and North America are creations by Daniel Chester French, who sculptured Lincoln for the Lincoln Memorial. In 1994 the Customs House opened as the **National Museum of the American Indian** ★ ★ *(212-825-6700. Adm. fee).* The regal interior spaces set the stage for the Smithsonian's Native American collection; it features permanent and changing exhibits. The essence of the holdings are masterworks by Indian artists. Discover virtuoso carvings from the Northwest, gold work from South America, and Southwestern Navajo weavings. Public programs highlight Indian music, dance, visual arts, and storytelling.

After heading south on Whitehall Street to the intersection with Water Street, you see the small **Peter Minuit Park**, which memorializes the shrewd Dutchman who bought Manhattan from native people. In this same area, look for **New York Unearthed** *(117 State St. 212-748-8628. April-Dec. Mon.-Sat., Jan.-March Mon.-Fri.)* if you want to view archaeological items from colonial New York. You can take an elevator that simulates a ride from Wall Street to the civilization that existed 400 years ago.

Walk a block east to Broad Street, then north to Pearl Street, to the tavern where George Washington made his farewell speech to his officers on December 4, 1783. ❺ **Fraunces Tavern** *(54 Pearl St. 212-425-1778)* is a brick Georgian building still vending grog and victuals—now to gangs of Wall Street traders. There is a small museum *(adm. fee)* with period rooms, including the Long Room, site of Washington's address.

New York's distant past fades as you walk north on Broad Street into Wall Street's skyscraper canyon. A district as well as a road, Wall Street takes its name from a wall the Dutch built in 1653. Spanning east to west across Lower Manhattan, it was erected as a

Getting Around Town

Yellow cabs dominate New York City streets, providing an excellent way to travel around town. But during rush hour, when the meter ticks 20 cents a minute for standing in traffic, cabs can become expensive—and excruciatingly slow. At these times, the fastest way to cover distance is the subway. Beefed-up security, refurbished stations, and modern cars with heat and air conditioning have gone a long way toward eliminating the subway's reputation as an urban frontier. Staying on track is not difficult if you pick up a free subway map at a token booth and remember that four lines run north to south— under Lexington Avenue, Sixth Avenue, Seventh Avenue/Broadway, and Eighth Avenue. Most trains stop at similar cross streets—among them 59th, 50th, 42nd, 34th, 23rd, and 14th. The Broadway and Lexington Avenue lines run to Battery Park, at the island's tip. If you plan to use the subway frequently, buy a roll of ten tokens. Subway trains run 24 hours a day. For more information call 718-330-1234.

13

Eighteenth-century room in Fraunces Tavern

defense against nearby Indians.

Amid the buildings of traditional financial houses, such as **Morgan Guaranty Trust Company** *(23 Wall St. at Broad St.)* and modern giants such as **Citibank** *(55 Wall St.),* stands the money pump called the **New York Stock Exchange** ★ *(20 Broad St. at Wall St. 212-656-5162. Mon.-Fri.).* Billions of dollars trade hands in this neoclassical temple with its facade of Corinthian columns. If you want to get up to the third-floor gallery to watch the trading, you must get free tickets, which the exchange releases each working morning at 9:05. Inside you find slides, videos, and guides to inform you about what looks like chaos below on the trading floor. Quite a change from the days when traders leaned against the trees or set up tables along "The Street" to conduct their business.

Diagonally across Wall Street stands another imperial-looking temple. **Federal Hall National Memorial** ★ *(26 Wall St. 212-825-6888. Mon.-Fri.)* emulates the Parthenon, and the statue of George Washington poised in front signals that this is the site where the general took the Oath of Office to become the first President of the United States. The museum inside has a self-guided tour and exhibitions on the U.S. Bill of Rights and Constitution. The steps are a favorite venue for the white shirts to smoke and snack on their lunch breaks.

Another sanctuary from the frenzy lies west of here, where Wall Street dead-ends at Broadway. ❻ **Trinity**

Hubbub at New York Stock Exchange

Church *(212-602-0872. Guided tours 2 p.m.)* stood as the tallest building in New York for part of the 19th century, but today this Anglican parish with its rose-colored Gothic chapel and graveyard look Lilliputian. Dating back more than 300 years, the cemetery makes a popular place for Wall Street denizens to escape for lunch. Pilgrim William Bradford, Alexander Hamilton, and Robert Fulton are buried here. There is a small museum, and classical concerts are offered most Thursdays at 1 p.m.

For the best aerial view of the city, head into the 5-acre **Tobin Plaza,** a favorite site for concerts, and enter the **World Trade Center** *(Bet. Liberty and Vesey Sts. 212-435-4170).* Go to the mezzanine level of Tower 2 to buy tickets for the 58-second elevator ride to the **Observation Deck**★★ *(212-323-2340. Adm. fee)* of this 1,350-foot building, the tallest in New York. Climb to the open-air observatory, the starting point for occasional stunts such as high wire walks between the two towers and skydiving.

To eat at the top of "the World," make reservations and dress up to dine at **Windows on the World**★★ *(212-524-7000).* The lower levels of the World Trade Center house a hotel, 60 shops and a **TKTS** *(Mezzanine, Tower 2. 212-768-1818. Mon.-Sat.)* outlet for half-price, same-day theater tickets. Head to the ninth floor of Building 4 to watch the **Commodities Exchange** *(212-748-1006. Sept.-May Mon.-Fri. Reservations required).*

Moving north on Broadway, you find the oldest continuous-use public building in the city, **St. Paul's Chapel** *(Bet. Fulton and Vesey Sts. 212-602-0872),* dating from 1766. Washington prayed here after his inauguration, and on Mondays you can sit near his pew as you enjoy a noontime classical concert *(donation).*

The **Woolworth Building**★ *(233 Broadway),* a block farther north, ranks as one of the most ornate skyscrapers in New York. This 60-story, neo-Gothic building is F.W. Woolworth's 1913 monument to his five-and-dime enterprise. The lobby with its soaring ceilings, marble walls, bronze furnishings, and murals is spectacular. Across the street in **❼ City Hall Park,** originally the town common (now a haven for chess players), sits the stately **City Hall**★ *(212-788-7171. Mon.-Fri. Group tours only).* Still the seat of New York City government, the small 1812 limestone palace mixes French Renaissance details with federal architecture. Still functioning after nearly two centuries, the building is worth a visit to escape the noise of the city and marvel at

15

Twin peaks of the World Trade Center

Dockside at South Street Seaport

Views of Brooklyn Heights

16

The subway, not the Empire State Building, is the key to the best panorama of Gotham. If you take the A or C train to the Brooklyn Bridge (High Street) stop just before sunset, your eyes will feast when you resurface in Brooklyn Heights, on the other side of the East River. To the west, all of Manhattan glows gold in the evening light as the shadows of the skyline stretch across the East River. A more athletic thrill is to stroll the East River Promenade along the brink of the Heights, and then head east along Montague Street to explore the federal-style brownstone town houses of the adjacent Brooklyn Heights Historic District.

the grandeur of the dome and spiraling staircases.

As you stroll down Nassau and Fulton Streets—partially closed to vehicles—you see that the neighborhood is changing. Nineteenth-century storefronts replace the skyscrapers of Wall Street. Ethnic restaurants and cafés with outdoor tables abound. Picking up the view of the East River and tall ships, you smell fish—a reminder that this 11-block **South Street Seaport Historic District**★★ *(212-732-7678)* remains the site of the working **Fulton Fish Market.**

Preservationists began buying up this neighborhood of federal-style counting houses, warehouses, and markets in 1967 to save Manhattan's historic waterfront from skyscraper development. But it took another twelve years before commercial interests such as the Rauch Corporation, which developed Boston's Quincy Market, reclaimed the district. The historic core of the seaport lies aboard the massive square-riggers **Peking** and **Wavertree** *(Pier 16. Adm. fee)* and other tall ships; and at **Schermerhorn Row,** a collection of 19th-century buildings housing shops, restaurants, taverns, and the **South Street Seaport Museum** *(Visitor Center, 12-14 Fulton St. 212-748-8600. Adm. fee)*. At the museum you can see exhibitions such as "Immigration in the Age of Sail" and obtain tickets for a summer sail aboard the schooner **Pioneer** *(May-Sept.; fare included in museum adm. fee. Reservations required)*.

The **❽ Fulton Market Building** *(Front and Fulton Sts.)* still has the fish market, located on the building's east side *(before sunrise)*. But there are lots of famous-name shops and restaurants in this restored building as well. With more of the same, the **Pier 17 Pavilion** models a 19th-century recreation pier. This is the place to pick from a collection of outdoor restaurants, including **Pedro O'Haras** *(212-227-6735)*, which overlooks the river, street entertainers, and the seaport's collection of tall ships. Sure the prices are a little steep...but where else will $3.75 buy you beer at a waterfront table overlooking the place your ancestors probably arrived full of dreams for this New World.

The Neighborhoods

● Walking tour ● 3 miles ● 1 day ● Year-round

Expect the unexpected when you go exploring in Greenwich Village and its surrounding neighborhoods—SoHo, Little Italy, and Chinatown. This walk on the wild side cruises the margins of New York that have been havens to generations of immigrants and bohemians. Starting at Washington Square Park in the heart of the Village, the route zigzags through enclaves of 19th-century buildings, a traditional Italian quarter, and the hip café-club-theater scene. In SoHo you'll find a National Historic District where 19th-century industrial buildings have evolved into an art scene of lofts and galleries. Then head to Little Italy to cruise restaurant row before crossing

Canal Street to enter Chinatown. The largest Asian community in the United States, it hums with street merchants and exotic sights and aromas.

Greenwich Village, usually described as the area below 14th Street, above Houston, from 4th Avenue and the Bowery to the Hudson River, is famed for its bohemian past—and present. Ask New Yorkers about the heart of the Village, ❶ **Washington Square Park**★

(Fifth Ave. and Washington Sq. N) and you are liable to hear something about its "weird energy." Spanning a number of city blocks, it is best identified by the memorial arch erected in 1889 for the centennial celebration of George Washington's inauguration. The original wood structure proved so popular it was replaced six years later by a marble version designed by Stanford White. Later statues of Washington were added (one of the sculptors was A. Stirling Calder, father of mobile artist Alexander Calder).

But the park began as a potter's field, and some say it still contains more than 10,000 graves. Public hangings and military drills were practiced here between 1797 and 1826, before the gentry moved in. The Greek Revival town houses on the north side were once home to New York high society, as described in Henry James's novel *Washington Square.* Authors who have called this area home include Edith Wharton and John Dos Passos, who wrote *Manhattan Transfer* in the 1920s behind No. 3 Washington Square North. By that time the Village had become a haunt for writers and artists.

Memorial arch at Washington Square Park

Today **New York University** mostly surrounds the park. Its Brown Building *(245 Greene St.)* is a former factory, site of the infamous Triangle Shirtwaist Fire of 1911. Commemorated each year by the New York Fire Department, the disaster killed 146 workers, mainly young immigrant girls, who were locked inside the building to prevent them from taking unauthorized breaks. Many of them jumped to their deaths. On the south side of the square the Loeb Student Center stands on the site of a boardinghouse nicknamed "the house of genius." It reputedly rented rooms to the likes of Stephen Crane, Willa Cather, and Eugene O'Neill. In the 1950s, the Beat Generation, led by Jack Kerouac and Allen Ginsberg, made the square their own, and Bob Dylan and a folk-singing crowd held court before the hippies and Vietnam War demonstrations took over. Currently, Washington Square Park seems an outlet for local kids, chess players, NYU students, dreamers, and counter-culture types.

Next, walk along West Fourth Street past ethnic eateries, vintage clothing vendors, and erotica shops. At Sheridan Square, site of violent riots involving freed slaves in 1863 and gay rights activists in 1969, cross Seventh Avenue and head west on **Christopher Street** ★, where the next two blocks of bars, shops, and theaters mark the heart of the gay community. An interesting stop is **McNulty's Tea & Coffee Co.** *(109 Christopher St. 212-242-5351),* which has been importing more than 200 varieties of tea since 1895. A fine off-Broadway theater is here as well, the **Lucille Lortel Theatre** *(121 Christopher St. 212-924-2817),* which produced the hit *Steel Magnolias.*

Italian bakery in SoHo

Just after turning south on Hudson Street, you will see ❷ **St. Luke-in-the-Fields** *(212-924-0562),* a federal-style church built in 1822, where Clement Clark Moore, who wrote the ballad *A Visit From St. Nicholas* (also known as *'Twas the Night Before Christmas*), served as a warden. You can imagine the past as you turn east on shady Grove Street and stroll by the clutch of federal town houses known as **Grove Court** *(Bet. Nos. 10-12 Grove St.).* Just a few steps away stands a building known as **Twin Peaks** *(102 Bedford St.),* a Roaring Twenties fantasy of mock Tudor architecture that came in response to conservative Village buildings. Back on Grove Street, take a look at No. 45, where poet Hart Crane spent his youth. No. 59 has a more somber air—this is where Thomas Paine died in 1809.

19

Reenergize at one of the many area restaurants, perhaps the southern-style **Pink Tea Cup** *(42 Grove St. 212-807-6755).* Then hit Seventh Avenue, where you might hear a rehearsal coming from one of the most famous jazz

Hanging out in Washington Square Park

clubs in the city, **Sweet Basil** *(88 Seventh Ave. S. 212-242-1785).* Turn down Barrow and onto Bedford, to **Chumley's** *(86 Bedford St. 212-675-4449),* a Prohibition-era speakeasy that remains quite hidden (there's no sign). It offers a working fireplace that is very welcoming to the hungry and thirsty on a raw day. At No. 75½ Bedford Street stands one of the narrowest residences in the city—9.5 feet wide—which was home of Pulitzer Prize-winner Edna St. Vincent Millay (1892-1950), whose poem "First Fig" begins with the sentiment many New Yorkers relate to, "My candle burns at both ends...." Nearby and recently renovated is the **Cherry Lane Theatre** (38 Commerce St. 212-989-2020), founded by Millay.

Return to Hudson Street and go south to **St. Lukes Place,** lined with 1850s Italianate row houses where many New York personalities have lived. Notice the two "mayor's lanterns" at No. 6, signifying the former residence of Mayor James J. "Jimmy" Walker, New York's charming but dishonest mayor who was forced to resign in 1932. Poet Marianne Moore lived at No. 14, and Theodore Dreiser rented the parlor floor of No. 19. But today's visitor is most likely to recognize No. 12, used as the exterior of the Huxtables' house in TV's *The Cosby Show.*

Continue along as St. Lukes Place becomes Leroy Street, cross Seventh Avenue, and join Bleecker Street. Here you'll find an old Italian neighborhood centered around ❸ **Father Demo Square,** where tenement buildings with outside fire escapes are the rule. For two blocks newsstands stocked with Italian papers, *grocerias* blaring Roman soccer on the radio, bakeries, and butcher shops give the city's best impression of life in this part of Manhattan, where one of the city's largest single ethnic waves of immigrants, 1.9 million Italians, hit the shore between 1899 and 1910.

The last leg of your Village walk explores the zone of cafés, bars, and small theaters clustered around the intersection of **Bleecker and MacDougal Streets ★ ★.** This is the scene that comes to mind when most people think of the Village—hip pedestrians, streetside cafés, and coffee houses such as **Caffe Borgia** (185 Bleecker St. 212-473-2290) and **Le Figaro** (184 Bleecker St. 212-677-1100). With the street sounds come chords of music from **The Bitter End** (147 Bleecker St. 212-673-7030) and its imitators. The laid-back lure of the Village is strong here, so pick a place to regroup and people-watch before moving on.

Cross south of Houston (HOW-ston) Street and enter **SoHo ★,** whose name is a clever shorthand for just that: the area SOuth of HOuston. A neighborhood of dying textile buildings 30 years ago, SoHo's vacant industrial lofts with their good light and open spaces began attracting artists. But it wasn't long until chic galleries, nouvelle cuisine restaurants, and film stars followed suit and by the

---

Welcome to America

A short side trip from Little Italy and Chinatown will take you to one of the most haunting sites in the city. The **Lower East Side Tenement Museum ★ ★** (90 Orchard St. 212-431-0233. Tues.-Fri., Sun.; adm. fee) has restored an 1863 tenement where you can picture how past waves of German, Jewish, and Italian immigrants lived after arriving in New York at the turn of the century. Today new Americans from Spanish-speaking countries, the Middle East, and Asia live in these tenement neighborhoods.

1980s, SoHo became the neighborhood of choice for New York's successful, creative types…and the struggling artists moved on.

Popularity has brought recognition as a National Historic District, restored SoHo's cast-iron style buildings, and made the streets safe. As you turn south on **Wooster Street,** look down at the Belgian-block street paving and up at the pastel-painted, tall warehouse buildings, with their large-windowed lofts. Streetside you'll stumble upon galleries, vintage clothing outlets, and vendors of all kinds of things. Stop in the **Dia Center for the Arts** *(141 Wooster St. 212-473-8072. Mid-Sept.–mid-June Wed.-Sat.),* where the second-floor **New York Earth Room** holds 140 tons of sculptured—you guessed it—earth.

The Pop Shop in SoHo

As you wander east along Prince Street, follow shoppers and artists into the **Dean & DeLuca Café** *(121 Prince St. 212-254-8776)* for a cappuccino (their main store, where you can purchase scrumptious specialty foods, is nearby on Broadway). Then turn the corner north on Broadway where the ❹ **Guggenheim Museum of SoHo**★ *(575 Broadway. 212-423-3878. Mon., Wed.-Sun.; donation)* is housed in a six-story restored cast-iron loft building, with rotating shows and works from the uptown museum's permanent collection. Amid the sea of galleries up the street, the **New Museum of Contemporary Art** *(583 Broadway. 212-219-1222. Wed.-Sun.; donation)* and the **Alternative Museum**★ *(594 Broadway. 212-966-4444. Tues.-Sat.; donation)* show some of the boldest and

Outdoor café in Little Italy

most controversial works from today's creative minds. Also of interest, the **Museum for African Art** *(593 Broadway. 212-966-1313. Closed Mon.; adm. fee)* features rotating exhibits that encompass carvings, textiles, masks, and sculptures.

You will see historic cast-iron-fronted buildings on Broadway, but to examine the best collection move south from Prince Street onto **Greene Street★,** where the block between Grand and Canal Streets contains an unbroken line of cast-iron oddities. In the mid-19th century, cast-iron buildings became popular for their ornamentation, easy construction, and load-bearing abilities without massive interior walls. These metal affairs showcased intricate architectural details—Italianate, neo-classical, or Gothic—formed of iron cast in standard molds. Take a close look at how No. 72, known as the **King of Greene Street,** mimics a Renaissance style with iron Corinthian columns.

A short walk east on Grand Street brings you to **Little Italy★.** Between the 1890s and 1920s, hundreds of thousands of Italian immigrants made their homes in the Lower East Side's so-called "railroad tenements"—with rooms strung out one to the next like a train. **Mulberry Street★** *(Bet. Broome and Canal Sts.)* remains the heart of the Italian enclave, but most Italians have moved out as the boundaries of Chinatown have crept north and SoHo has progressed from the west. Today, Little Italy consists of just a few blocks of *ristorantes, caffès,* and trattorias, but these are not easily passed by. Stop in for a cannoli at

Caffe Roma *(Broome and Mulberry Sts. 212-226-8413)*, or a pizza and *bruschetta* at the **Italian Food Center** *(Grand and Mulberry Sts. 212-925-2954)*. Or just wander around and let your nose decide where to dine. If it is near September 19, you can get a real feel for the old country when the Feast of San Gennaro turns Mulberry Street into a huge block party.

Walking past **Canal Street** and through the endless line of noodle shops, Chinese vegetable stands, ideograms on signs, and row upon row of street vendors selling counterfeit watches, you might think you have landed in Hong Kong. In **Chinatown★,** the harmonies of Cantonese and pentatonic music fills your ears, and the scent of ginger filters through the air. Once a much smaller neighborhood, Chinatown now houses perhaps 200,000 people of Asian descent and it continues to grow. As you walk the streets, look up to windows on the upper floors of the buildings and listen to the hum of sewing machines. Hundreds of garment-making businesses provide ready employment for recent arrivals from Asia…just as they did for the Europeans before them.

To get a sense of the richness and diversity of these people, seek out the ❺ **Museum of Chinese in the Americas★** *(70 Mulberry St., 2nd fl. 212-619-4785. Tues.-Sat.; adm. fee)*. Here exhibits include origami made by the *Golden Venture* refugees whose ship ran aground off New York in 1993, as well as photos and narratives about Chinese Americans in World War II. This is also the place to pick up a map and brochure on Chinatown, or to join a walking tour.

To complete your walk, explore **Mott Street★★,** Chinatown's traditional community center. Tempting restaurants await, but if sweets are your thing, go for the walnut-almond cookies at **Lung Fong Bakery** *(41 Mott St.*

Chinatown market

212-233-7447). For a respite, stop in at the **Eastern States Buddhist Temple of America** *(64 Mott St.)* and experience the "serenity that passeth understanding" in the presence of more than 100 statues of Buddha. Or lose yourself amid the nodding straw hats, swaying bamboo fans, and clatter of shoe cobblers on narrow **Doyer Street,** one-time haunt of opium dealers.

● **Walking tour** ● **2 miles** ● **One day** ● **Year-round**

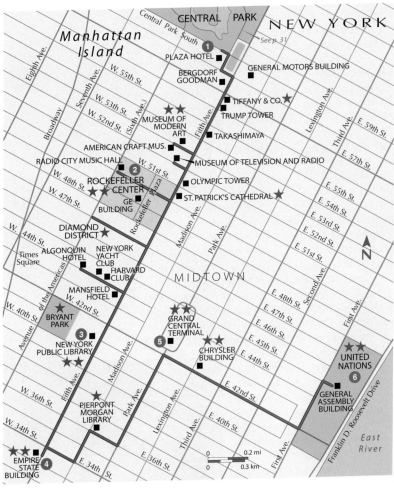

Jam-packed with skyscrapers, Midtown bristles with the energy of a world-class business district. During rush hour, hordes of workers form a smooth, unstoppable sea, adding to the hectic pace that typifies this part of Manhattan. Home to powerful companies, chic boutiques, and fascinating museums, the area is doubly impressive when you consider that very little of what you see existed a century ago. This walk begins at the Plaza Hotel on Central Park South, and heads south on Fifth Avenue, arguably the most famous street in the world. You will pass top-of-the-line stores such as FAO Schwarz and Tiffany & Co., along with the fanciful Trump Tower.

The Museum of Modern Art and other nearby museums make for engaging side stops before continuing on down Fifth Avenue to St. Patrick's Cathedral and Rockefeller Center. Here, you can break from the crowds and duck into the shops of the Diamond District, then call a time-out at the New York Public Library or a nearby café. The Empire State Building, with its observatory, will mark your next stop. Finally, you travel east to visit Grand Central Terminal, the Chrysler Building, and the United Nations.

A National Historic Landmark, the ❶ **Plaza Hotel** *(Central Park S. at Fifth Ave. 212-759-3000 or 800-759-3000)* reigns as the queen of Fifth Avenue. Built in the style of a Renaissance château, the hotel has hosted the rich and famous for nearly a hundred years. With horse-drawn carriages near its entrance, colorful flags, and spiffy doormen, the Plaza paints a picture of sophistication. Elegant diners slink into the Palm Court or the more intimate Oak Room. Pass through the lobby to see the painting of "Eloise" *(near the Central Park S. entrance)*, the fictional imp who romped through the hotel in Kay Thompson's charming children's book. Browse some of the shops and savor the lavish atmosphere.

Across Fifth Avenue, the 50-story **General Motors Building** houses the world's ultimate toy store, **FAO Schwarz**★ *(767 Fifth Ave. 212-644-9400)*. Tom Hanks tap-danced his way through a scene in *Big* here, and more than a few

The Big Apple

The nickname was coined by 1920s jazz musicians—it was their way of designating New York as the ultimate venue for a performer. And how! New York's five boroughs swell with more than 7.3 million people. There are 59,000 hotel rooms and 17,000 eating establishments to choose from in Manhattan. Over three quarters of a million people commute to work in Midtown, 25 million "out-of-towners" visit each year, and 35 Broadway theaters host over 9 million people yearly.

25

Midtown Manhattan skyscrapers

Trump Tower's gilded escalators

visitors may feel the urge to repeat the caper amid the super-size stuffed animals.

Adult collections await at the king of Midtown's upscale department stores, **Bergdorf Goodman** *(754 Fifth Ave. 212-753-7300)*, where Cornelius Vanderbilt II's mansion stood before the skyscraper craze brought an end to the palatial houses that gave Fifth Avenue the nickname "Millionaires' Row."

The corner of 57th Street and Fifth Avenue tempts everyone who loves style and luxury. **Burberrys** *(9 E. 57th St. 212-371-5010)* has added to its array of stylish outerwear; **CHANEL** *(15 E. 57th St. 212-355-5050)* recently moved here and expanded its salon of fashion and scent; and **Tiffany & Co.** ★ *(727 Fifth Ave. 212-755-8000)* showcases fabulous jewelry in display windows and greets customers with impeccable courtesy.

As you proceed down Fifth Avenue, you see one of the newer additions to the skyline, **Trump Tower** *(725 Fifth Ave. 212-832-2000)*. Built in 1983, the black tower features a 6-story atrium of pink marble and polished brass. There are classic shops here such as **Cartier,** along with piped-in trumpet music and a waterfall. The upper floors include offices and condominiums.

Takashimaya *(693 Fifth Ave. 212-350-0100)*, one of Japan's largest retailers, is a newcomer on this avenue whose international élan came from European stars such as **Christian Dior** *(703 Fifth Ave. 212-223-4646)*...until recently. The 20-story building opened in 1993, featuring American and Asian arts and crafts, household accessories, and furnishings. While you are in the neighborhood you might want to detour west on 55th Street to **J.P.'s French Bakery** ★ *(54 W. 55th St. 212-765-7575)* for what some people claim to be the best croissants in the city.

On West 53rd Street you will find one of the highlights of Midtown—the **Museum of Modern Art (MoMA)** ★★ *(Bet. 5th and 6th Aves. 212-708-9480. Closed Wed.; adm. fee)*. The museum was founded in 1929 and moved into its present quarters in 1939. Always controversial, MoMA hired architect Cesar Pelli in the early 1980s to add a 44-story condo tower to generate income. Purists lament the tower, but everyone enjoys the expanded galleries with glass walls overlooking the **Sculpture Garden.** Now, visitors can see rooms devoted to Picasso and Matisse and paintings such as van Gogh's *Starry Night* and Andrew Wyeth's *Christina's World*. The photography collection is second to none, and you can see classic films in an ongoing series.

Across the street stands the **MoMA Design Store** *(44 W. 53rd St. 212-708-9669)*, which sells elegant objects for home and office; and the **American Craft Museum** *(40 W. 53rd St. 212-956-3535. Closed Mon.; adm. fee)*, a humorous showcase for clay, metal, wood, glass, and fiber creations.

If you feel nostalgic for reruns of the old radio show *Amos and Andy* or the TV series *All in the Family*, stop at the **Museum of Television and Radio** *(25 W. 52nd St. 212-621-6600. Closed Mon.; donation)*. Two theaters, screening rooms, and listening stations give nonstop entertainment, while the galleries have exhibits such as masks from *Star Wars*.

A sanctuary of a different sort awaits at Fifth Avenue and 51st Street. Dating from the 1870s, the French Gothic-style **St. Patrick's Cathedral** ★ *(212-753-2261)* is among the world's largest churches. With its 330-foot spires, 70 stained-glass windows, and flickering votive candles, the cathedral transports visitors light-years from Fifth Avenue. For an ironic touch, look for the church's reflection in the black glass of the **Olympic Tower** next door.

Across the street stands ❷ **Rockefeller Center** ★★ *(Bet. 5th and 6th Aves., W. 51st to W. 48th Sts. 212-632-3975)*, which blankets 21 prime Manhattan acres with 19 buildings, including **Radio City Music Hall** *(1260 6th Ave. 212-632-4041)*, a venue for top performers. John D. Rockefeller II began building the world's largest privately owned business-entertainment enclave in 1928. In addition to a sunken plaza that holds a skating rink in winter and an open-air restaurant in summer, the center also contains a barber shop, a post office, public rest rooms—and New York City's famous gigantic Christmas

27

Taking in Tom Wesselmann's *Smoker, 1 (Mouth, 12)*, at MoMA

tree. In many ways it really is New York's town square.

To grasp the size and history here, head for the **GE Building** *(30 Rockefeller Plaza)*, the limestone-and-aluminum tower overlooking the sunken plaza. At the information desk sign up for a free tour of the complex. Pick up maps and brochures about the center's history. You may have to wait in line, but you can get tickets here for **NBC Studio Tours** and shows such as *Saturday Night Live (212-664-4000. Adm. fee)*. Katie Couric and company broadcast the *Today Show* from the picture-window studio on the street. The **Rainbow Room** *(212-632-5100)* in the GE Building remains one of the country's most celebrated top-floor dining experiences.

One block south, take a side trip to New York's **Diamond District**★ *(W. 47th St. bet. 5th and 6th Aves.)*. Thousands of dealers—many of whom are Hasidic Jews with beards, side curls, and black hats—fill the little shops on this street, conducting as much as 85 percent of America's wholesale gem trade. Stop in any of these shops to buy (or fantasize about) an expensive souvenir.

If you want to peek into the world of New York's gentry, take a stroll down West 44th Street. This block includes the Harvard Club *(27 W. 44th St. Private)* and the New York Yacht Club *(37 W. 44th St. Private)*, where second-floor windows mimic the stern of a Dutch vessel. You can dine or have a drink at the **Algonquin Hotel** *(59 W. 44th St. 212-840-6800)*, which is where Dorothy Parker and Robert Benchley held forth at the famous literary round table in the 1920s (the table, as well as the Rose Room, where they met, are long gone). Book a room in the **Mansfield Hotel** *(12 W. 44th St. 212-944-6050)*, a classic boutique accommodation, if you want full immersion in the genteel lifestyle.

When the city gets to be too much for Midtowners, they often head for the ❸ **New York Public Library**★★ *(Bet. W. 42nd and W. 40th Sts. 212-869-8089. Closed Sun.; tours)*. Just climbing the steps between the lion statues of *Patience* and *Fortitude* can be a liberat-

28

Statue of Prometheus at Rockefeller Center skating rink

ing experience as the crowds fade below and the marble facade of this beaux arts temple welcomes you. Undergoing extensive restoration, the library's high ceilings, statues, and carvings inspire serenity in Astor Hall. But beneath the tranquility serious enterprises are afoot. With more than 17 million items, this building is one of the world's largest research libraries, and its stacks run for 125 miles. Don't miss Gilbert Stuart's portrait of George Washington in Room 316.

You wouldn't know it by looking at the large formal garden in neighboring **Bryant Park★,** but many of the library's stacks lie beneath the turf. The site of America's first World Fair in 1853, Bryant Park earned a seedy reputation after the homeless and unemployed began gathering here during the Depression; it did not lose it until a commission restored the park in the late 1980s. Today, the park hosts a series of community events, including an outdoor summer film series. An outdoor café provides a quiet respite in summer.

29

Radio City Music Hall

Walking south on Fifth Avenue again, you can't miss your next stop looming above the corner of West 34th Street. The 1,454-foot tower of the ❹ **Empire State Building★★** *(350 Fifth Ave.)* is a New York landmark, the site of romantic scenes in *An Affair to Remember* and *Sleepless in Seattle.* The world's tallest building when it opened in 1931, the Empire State now ranks third...but that doesn't stop the flow of tourists—over 3.5 million a year. On most days lines begin to form for the Observatories *(212-736-3100. Adm. fee)* before they open, and you could spend more than an hour waiting for a trip to the 86th floor open deck and the 102nd floor lookout. Some tourists opt for the New York Skyride *(212-564-2224. Adm. fee),* a simulated helicopter tour around the city.

Leaving the Empire State Building, veer east on 34th Street, then north on Madison Avenue. Shade trees and turn-of-the-century mansions soften the city's modern face before you reach the Italian palazzo housing the **Pierpont Morgan Library★** *(29 E. 36th St. 212-685-0610. Closed Mon.;*

adm. fee). The famous banker J.P. Morgan collected rare books, illuminated manuscripts, and drawings. Here you can sit and wonder at rarities such as a Gutenberg Bible, view Morgan's personal study, or relax in a garden café.

Walk a block east to Park Avenue and stroll up to the front doors of one of the great palaces of transportation, the mammoth, beaux arts-style ❺ **Grand Central Terminal**★★ *(E. 42nd St. and Park Ave. 212-532-4900 or 800-METRO-INFO)*. Suffering constant use since its opening in 1913, Grand Central has recently been undergoing massive renovations—a pet project of the late Jacqueline Kennedy Onassis—to revive the beauty of the 60-foot windows, gigantic sculptures, vaulted ceilings, and marble concourses. Metro North trains depart from here today, but the bronze figure of Cornelius Vanderbilt on the southern facade recalls the era when the station was the imperial seat of his New York Central Railroad.

East on 42nd Street, you will see one last monument to commerce and ego. The facade of the **Chrysler Building**★★ *(405 Lexington Ave.)* incorporates different parts of Chrysler automobiles. Considered the ultimate in art deco styling, the Chrysler was the world's tallest building for two years, until the Empire State Building nosed it out in 1931. But what the Chrysler lost in height, it gained with boldness. Both outside and in, step back and try to count the dozens of design frills that mimic automobile styling.

Security Council chamber, United Nations

Tranquility is elusive in Midtown, but the world strives for peace a few blocks east. Since its construction shortly after World War II, the ❻ **United Nations**★★ *(E. 45th St. and First Ave. 212-963-1234. Adm. fee)* has become a symbol of world peace and multicultural harmony. Once the site of Turtle Bay, the U.N.'s 18 acres are designated as international territory. The arched-roof General Assembly Building and the glass-fronted Secretariat Building are familiar sights, along with the flapping flags of 180 member nations. To learn about the struggle for world peace, enter through the 46th Street gate, go to the General Assembly Building, pass through a security check, and head for the information desk. But if you want immediate serenity, walk into the rose garden overlooking the East River and let the wind carry your worries away.

Museum Mile

- ● **Walking tour** ● **1.5 miles**
- ● **2 days** ● **Year-round**

Roughly bordered by Fifth Avenue and Central Park, New York City's "Museum Mile" beckons with some of the world's finest museums—the Frick Collection, the Whitney Museum of American Art, the Metropolitan Museum of Art, and the Guggenheim. An interplay between art and nature, this walking tour weaves in and out of Central Park to visit these rich cultural repositories, along with some lesser-known delights. Along the way, enjoy the great park's wooded valleys, placid ponds, and wide-open lawns, ideal for sunbathing or people watching. Twisted paths lead to such natural splendors as the Shakespeare Garden and the often overlooked Conservatory Garden—one of Central Park's treasures.

The Plaza Hotel, located across from Central Park's southeast entrance at E. 59th Street, owes some of its glamour to ❶ **Grand Army Plaza**★ and the Pulitzer Fountain, which are bisected by Central Park South between E. 60th and E. 58th Streets. Brightened by flower beds in warm months, the plaza creates an open-air space free from skyscrapers, where you can step back and admire the Plaza's Renaissance facade and the adjacent parklands. Top-hatted drivers line up horse-drawn carriages here, waiting to lead romantics on a slow-moving jaunt through the park. Funds for the fountain, dominated by the female incarnation of *Abundance,* were donated by publisher Joseph Pulitzer.

As soon as you enter **Central Park**★★, bear left and follow the path down to **The Pond**★. Once swan boats plied this crescent-shaped basin;

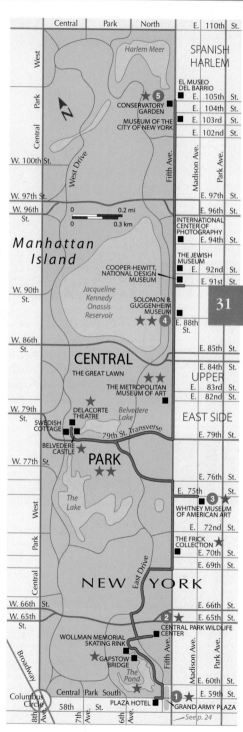

31

View from the Lake, Central Park

today ducks have the run of the place. Walk across **Gapstow Bridge★,** at the pond's northern end, to admire the reflection of Midtown's skyline on still waters. Here, city sounds vanish beneath the music emanating from nearby **Wollman Memorial Skating Rink** *(212-396-1010. Call for schedule; adm. fee),* where, according to season, ice skaters and roller-bladers strut their stuff.

Lingering on the bridge, ponder the miracle of Central Park. Once a wasteland of hog farms and squatter settlements, the 843-acre park was created in response to a design competition in 1855 for a new public sanctuary. Journalist Frederick Law Olmsted and architect Calvert Vaux submitted their "Greensward Plan," which won. Development moved slowly over the next 16 years, but in the end the sanctuary achieved Olmsted's goal of creating a place where city dwellers could escape the city.

Kissing a seal,
Central Park Wildlife Center

Strolling up the park's eastern side, you quickly come to the ❷ **Central Park Wildlife Center★** *(212-861-6030. Adm. fee),* popularly known as the zoo. Fanning out from the sea lion pool—whose playful residents always attract a crowd—are exhibits featuring tropical, temperate, and polar environments. The café just outside the zoo entrance makes a good stop for a coffee break.

Now walk northeast along East Drive, where you

share the shade and birdsong with travelers in passing carriages. After a short walk, exit the park at E. 69th Street and continue north along Fifth Avenue to the **Frick Collection** ★ *(1 E. 70th St. 212-288-0700. Closed Mon.; adm. fee).* Henry Clay Frick, the chairman of the Carnegie Steel Corporation, built this beaux arts mansion in 1914 with the express purpose of showcasing his eclectic collection of Old Masters from the 14th through 19th centuries. Sunny, baronial rooms off a glass-covered courtyard contain well-known works by Bellini, Goya, Renoir, Vermeer, Rembrandt, El Greco, Van Dyck, and more. The Frick feels like a lavish private home, decorated with its owner's favorite objects. Titian's *Man in a Red Cape* is here, as is Rembrandt's *The Polish Rider.*

Continuing north on Fifth Avenue and jogging east on E. 75th Street, you come to the ❸ **Whitney Museum of American Art** ★ *(Madison Ave. and 75th St. 212-570-3676. Wed.-Sun.; adm. fee).* Standing in bold contrast to the Frick mansion, the Whitney is a forbidding, Bauhaus-style, granite castle that you enter across a moat. Wealthy sculptor Gertrude Vanderbilt Whitney began a mission in 1930 to attract attention to American artists, and she pulled together a collection of her contemporaries— George Bellows, Thomas Hart Benton, Edward Hopper, and Georgia O'Keeffe, among others. Drawing on its 10,000-piece collection of contemporary art, sculpture, and painting, the Whitney runs changing shows. The screening of controversial independent American films and videos is a example of the institution's place in the avant garde.

For some fresh air and a walk in the park, retrace your steps to Fifth Avenue. Enter Central Park at E. 76th Street and wind your way northwest toward what looks like a Scottish fortress on a hill. Built in 1872 of schist commonly found in the park, **Belvedere Castle** ★ *(212-772-0210. Closed Mon.)* was designed as a scenic monument capping Vista Rock and overlooking Belvedere Lake. The castle functions as an observatory for the National Weather Service; inside you can see displays on the service, as well as participate in hands-on naturalist programs.

The castle's height offers the park's best vistas. From here you look down on the **Great Lawn,** where a free summer concert series draws 500,000 people to hear such music legends as Luciano Pavarotti. The castle also overlooks the open-air stage of the **Delacorte Theater** ★ *(212-861-7277. June-Sept. Tues.-Sun.),* where

Not Your Average Village Green

While the landscape of Central Park might look like a wilderness preserve, construction crews, beginning in 1858, moved millions of cubic yards of earth to create this topography, and added dozens of species of trees and shrubs. There are 58 miles of trails and more than a half-dozen artificial bodies of water. Today, the park is an oasis for over 200 species of birds...and a retreat for walking, jogging, cycling, roller-blading, skating, boating, sunning, horseback riding, tennis, softball, folk dancing, and concerts. More than 15 million people share the park each year, making it a generally safe environment, particularly on weekends, when half the city seems at play. Avoiding night visits and isolated areas is the best way to ensure you won't be a target for desperate people.

33

Shakespeare is performed each summer under the stars. The plays are free, but you need a ticket. People start lining up at the ticket office long before it opens at 1 p.m. To assure tickets, bring a picnic lunch and join the hundreds of others waiting in line.

You can find peace and quiet at the nearby **Shakespeare Garden,** planted with vegetation the bard mentions in his plays. The nearby **Swedish Cottage** *(212-988-9093. Oct.-June Tues.-Sat., July-Sept. Mon.-Fri.; fee for performances. Reservations required),* a wooden chalet, was imported from Sweden for the 1876 Centennial Exposition in Philadelphia; it now serves as a puppet theater.

Exiting the park to Fifth Avenue at E. 79th Street, you find yourself at the southern corner of New York's most visited building, and the Western Hemisphere's largest art museum: the **Metropolitan Museum of Art**★★ *(82nd St. and Fifth Ave. 212-879-5500.*

Angel of the Waters fountain, Central Park

Closed Mon.; adm. fee). Hosting five million people a year, the Met's halls, wings, and annexes cover 2 million square feet. And yet, only a third of the museum's nearly three million objects are on display at any given time. It's almost inconceivable that this institution began less than 130 years ago, with fewer than 200 works of art. Over the years, the wealthy—the Morgans, Rockefellers, Lehmans, Sacklers—have made their claims on immortality, attaching their names to wings, galleries, and collections.

You feel humility and excitement as you climb the imposing stairs leading to the columned beaux arts facade. Entering through the spectacular **Great Hall,** stop at the Information Desk for a floor plan and ask about guided or

34

tape-recorded tours, gallery talks, and other special activities.

One of the Met's traditional strengths has been its antiquities, and high on many people's lists are the **Egyptian Galleries** ★★, which not only include 3,000 years of art, but also the **Temple of Dendur,** a first-century B.C. temple and gate overlooking a reflecting pool. Check out the **Michael C. Rock-**

Temple of Dendur, Metropolitan Museum of Art

efeller Wing for the art of Africa, Oceania, and the Americas; and the **Astor Garden,** modeled after a Ming scholar's garden. And that's just a beginning. Linger for hours in the world's largest collection of American art, featuring works by Copley, Homer, Sargent, and Cassatt. Or head to the European painting galleries to admire room after room of Vermeer, Rembrandt, Gainsborough, Raphael, Botticelli, Velázquez, Monet, and Cézanne; here you'll find El Greco's *View of Toledo* and Rembrandt's *Aristotle with a Bust of Homer.*

And then there are the musical instruments from around the world, the period rooms in the American wing that portray more than two dozen historical eras, the armor belonging to medieval knights and horses, the sculpture garden filled with Rodin bronzes, and the list goes on.

Pause for a refreshing drink on the open-air **Roof Garden** *(May–late fall, weather permitting),* with the city as the backdrop. Weekend evenings often feature a classical quartet, candlelit tables, and a bar above the Great Hall…which many people consider to be the perfect prelude to dinner on the town.

Continue your tour by walking four blocks north on Fifth Avenue to the ❹ **Solomon R. Guggenheim Museum** ★★ *(1071 Fifth Ave. 212-360-3500. Closed Thurs.; adm. fee).* In a city that relishes bold architecture, the Guggenheim building has never lost its power to dazzle and offend. Designed by Frank Lloyd Wright in the 1940s, the Guggenheim's interior core is an outward spiraling ramp of alabaster concrete that twists six stories in the air to a glass dome. Clearly a flight of fancy, the structure reminds some of a beehive. The art that hangs along the ramps and throughout the adjoining galleries is just as provocative. The Guggenheim's collection favors abstract paintings by the likes of Kandinski, Mondriaan, Klee, and Kline, which you'll find in the Thannhauser galleries, adjacent to the main spiral gallery. Here, too, hang the paintings of well-known Cubists, including Picasso, as well as works by photographer Robert Mapplethorpe.

36

GUGGENHEIM MUSEUM

Guggenheim Museum by Frank Lloyd Wright

The main gallery features changing exhibits of modern and contemporary art.

Walking 2 blocks north on Fifth Avenue, you discover a place where "design" has just as high a priority as at the Guggenheim…but a very different style. Part of the Smithsonian Institution, the **Cooper-Hewitt, National Design Museum** *(E. 91st St., off Fifth Ave. 212-860-6868. Closed Mon.; adm. fee)* resides in the 64-room Georgian mansion of the late steel tycoon Andrew Carnegie (see sidebar p. 102). Galleries showcase jewelry, glass, metal, ceramics, furniture, and textiles—a stunning collection started by the three Hewitt sisters, whose wealth stemmed from their inventor-industrialist grandfather, Peter Cooper. In the late 1960s, the collection was transferred to the care of the Smithsonian Institution, and the mansion was acquired from the Carnegie Corporation to house it. Before a 20-million-dollar renovation in 1995, visitors often came here more for the house and garden tour than the art; today's new exhibits give the collection equal billing.

Before heading north, cross the street and enter the park at E. 90th Street to view the lovely **Reservoir** *(E. 90th St.),* which is lined with a 1.6-mile jogging path. Now walk one block up Fifth Avenue to a dramatic French-Gothic château, harking back to Fifth Avenue's turn-of-the-century glory. The former home of Felix and

Frieda Warburg, the 1908 mansion has housed the **Jewish Museum** *(E. 92nd St. and Fifth Ave. 212-423-3230. Sun.-Thurs.; adm. fee)* since 1947. The first two floors display rotating exhibits by well-known Jewish artists including George Segal. On the upper two floors you'll discover outstanding displays covering 4,000 years of Jewish culture, featuring hundreds of pieces from the museum's 27,000-article permanent collection.

A smaller mansion at E. 94th Street and Fifth Avenue holds the **International Center of Photography** *(1130 Fifth Ave. 212-860-1777. Closed Mon.; adm. fee)*. Founded in 1974, the ICP displays revolving exhibits of works by world-renowned photographers, including Capa, Cartier-Bresson, Atget, Riboud, and Stieglitz. The museum labs bustle with workshops year-round.

If your travels through the Big Apple have left you with a fragmented sense of New York City's history, you can put it all into perspective by continuing north on Fifth Avenue about ten blocks to the **Museum of the City of New York** *(1220 Fifth Ave. 212-534-1672. Wed.-Sun.; donation)*. Galleries full of paintings, Tiffany silver, fire-fighting equipment, and costumes provide a fascinating glimpse into three centuries of the city's past. In the New York City Community Gallery, you'll find changing exhibits and programs developed by the museum and other not-for-profit, community-based groups that explore the city's diverse culture.

Carved hand, El Museo del Barrio

The last museum on your tour stands just a block north, but is often overlooked. **El Museo del Barrio** *(1230 Fifth Ave. 212-831-7272. Wed.-Sun.; donation)* began in 1969 as a neighborhood showplace of local Puerto Rican artists living in nearby Spanish Harlem. The museum has grown to include both historic and contemporary artwork from Latin America.

New Yorkers say you really can't claim to know the city's pleasures without passing into Central Park through the iron gates that stand virtually across the street from El Museo, at 105th Street. Here you enter into the ❺ **Conservatory Garden** ★ *(212-860-1382. Adm. fee)*, several formal gardens (including Italian and French) dotted with fountains, a lily pond, and a pergola, and filled with flowering crabapple trees and wisteria. A planting of 20,000 tulips heralds the arrival of spring. The hedge-rimmed perennial Secret Garden, named for the children's classic, makes just the kind of place you might imagine pausing to create some art of your own.

Long Island Idyll★

● **105 miles** ● **3 days** ● **Spring and autumn**

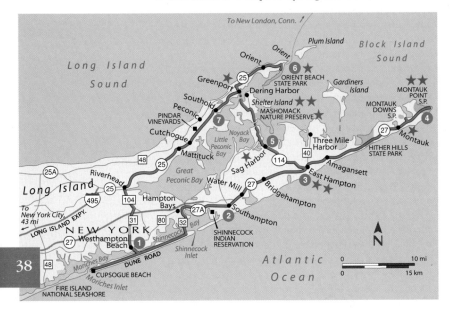

There's a secret to enjoying Long Island: Come during the sunny days in spring or autumn, when the summer vacation crowd is not in force. You'll have the quaint streets and beaches practically to yourself. The drive enters this land of leisure from New York City, stopping at a few historic residences before heading out to the diverse houses of Westhampton Beach and then Southampton, where estates reminiscent of *The Great Gatsby* stretch down to the beach for miles around, making it a playground of film stars, artists, and Manhattan's upper crust. The island then splits into two peninsulas. The South Fork offers windswept

Southampton summer residence

Montauk, dominated by dunes, sportfishing boats, state parks, and the historic whaling port of Sag Harbor. A ferry ride leads to rural Shelter Island, from which another goes to Greenport on Long Island's North Fork. This latter area is as rustic as the South Fork is chic, with a maritime museum, a tall ship, and a traditional seaport. The drive moves east among farms and historic villages to the tip of the North Fork at Orient Point. Here, a state park recalls Long Island much as it was after glaciers retreated some 45,000 years ago. The final leg of the trip runs west through Cutchogue, where vineyards are replacing potato farms.

Heading out from New York City on the Long Island Expressway (I-495), you may want to break up the trip with a detour to **Westbury House and Gardens** ★ *(71 Old Westbury Rd., Old Westbury. 516-333-0048. May-Oct.; adm. fee).* The estate of financier John S. Phipps, the house contains a fine collection of paintings and 18th-century furniture, while the gardens are a delight. Another worthwhile side trip is Oyster Bay's **Sagamore Hill National Historic Site** *(20 Sagamore Hill Rd. 516-922-4447. Adm. fee),* the house Theodore Roosevelt helped to design upon his graduation from Harvard in 1884. It served as his main residence for the rest of his life, as well as his summer White House. Many original furnishings remain, as well as exhibits on Roosevelt's accomplishments. Also consider stopping at **Old Bethpage Village Restoration** *(Round Swamp Rd., Old Bethpage. 516-572-8400. Wed.-Sun., closed Jan.-Feb.; adm. fee),* where costumed interpreters welcome you to a complex of restored mid-19th-century buildings.

Then make your way back to I-495, exiting onto N.Y. 25 and County Rds. 104 and 31 to ❶ **Westhampton Beach** *(Chamber of Commerce 631-288-3337).* A warm weather retreat since P.T. Barnum summered here in the late 1860s, the town looks like just another prosperous suburb...until you cross the drawbridge to **Dune Road.** Here, beach houses, in grandiose styles from Italianate to beaux arts to classic New England farmhouse, crown the barrier island dunes stretching more than 20 miles from Moriches Inlet to Shinnecock Inlet. Beach access is difficult here, unless you head to **Cupsogue Beach** *(631-852-8111. Parking fee mid-June–mid-Sept.),* at the very west end of Dune Road.

Leave the island to the east on County Rd. 32 and drive around Shinnecock Bay, a focal point for boaters and fishermen because of its marinas, ocean inlet, and the canal that cuts across the South Fork to Great Peconic Bay. Stop for lunch along the canal's edge and watch the

Fire Island

Divided from Long Island by Great South Bay, more than 30 miles of barrier beach, marsh, sunken forest, and bay islands stand in contrast to Long Island's heavy development. During its early history, **Fire Island National Seashore** *(631-289-4810)* served as an outpost for whalers and the Life-saving Service. Vacationers discovered the island in the mid-1800s, and by the middle of the 20th century a proposed highway promised to overwhelm its fragile ecosystem with throngs of sun-worshiping weekenders. After much lobbying from local communities and environmental groups, the land became protected as a national seashore in 1964. Popular among swimmers, beach walkers, and anglers, Fire Island can be reached via the Robert Moses Causeway near West Islip, passenger ferries from Sayville or Patchogue, and the William Floyd Parkway at Shirley. No driving is allowed on the island; cars must be parked in lots *(fee).*

39

Fishing near Montauk Point Lighthouse

coming and going of sportfishing boats where the Shinnecock Indians made their canoe portages, now occupied by the 1750 **Canoe Place Inn** *(631-728-4121)*.

Follow N.Y. 27A farther east around the bay past the **Shinnecock Indian Reservation** *(N.Y. 27A. 631-287-2460)*, where you can experience a pow wow *(adm. fee)* if you want to risk the crowds on Labor Day. As you continue east, notice the contrast between the undeveloped forest and hills of the Indian land and the estates lining the road as you enter ❷ **Southampton** *(Chamber of Commerce 631-283-0402)*. The heart of the "fashionable Hamptons," this village is a collection of turn-of-the-century summer mansions dressed in cedar shingles or white clapboards and tucked behind tall hedges and security gates. The rich and famous began summering here in the 1890s, and they haven't left. To see some of their houses, go south on First Neck Lane, then east on Gin Lane. There are also beach access roads here with parking spaces, although you need a parking permit in the summer; a season pass is available from Town Hall *(116 Hampton Rd. 631-283-6000)*.

This town traces its roots to English colonists who arrived here from Massachusetts in 1640. To gain a better

understanding of the history, head into town to the
Southampton Museum★ *(17 Meeting House Ln. 631-283-2494. Mid-June–mid-Sept. Tues.-Sun.; adm. fee)*. You can tour a
complex of 12 buildings here, including a whaling captain's home, a blacksmith's shop, and a tavern. The **Parrish Art Museum** *(25 Job's Ln. 631-283-2118. Closed
Tues.-Wed. mid-Sept.–May; donation)* calls attention to the
town's prominence as an artist colony, with changing
shows and work by such 19th- and 20th-century artists as
impressionists William Merrit Chase and Fairfield Porter
and modern masters Jackson Pollock and Willem de
Kooning, who were drawn to the Hampton's crisp light.

Continue east on what now becomes the South Fork's
main artery, N.Y. 27, to the town of **Water Mill** and the
Water Mill Museum *(Old Mill Rd. 631-726-4625. Mid-May–Sept.; adm. fee)*, where the wheel has been turning to
grind grain, spin yarn, weave cloth, and make paper
since the 1720s. The mill sets the scene for a rural flavor
that begins to permeate the region as you move east.
Farmstands and three new vineyards appear at roadside,
and gentry on horseback are not uncommon.

Along this route are two villages dating back to the

17th century, ❸ **East Hampton**★★ *(Chamber of Commerce 631-324-0362)* and neighboring **Amagansett.** Not so obviously opulent but every bit as full of the rich and famous as Southampton, these communities have focused much effort on historic preservation, evident by a stroll around the historic district near the pond in the town center. The **East Hampton Historical Society** *(101 Main St. 631-324-6850)* operates several sites along Main Street, including the 1784 **Clinton Academy** *(151 Main St.),* the state's first chartered academy; the 1680 **Mulford Farm** *(10 James Ln.),* a living history museum portraying the original East Hampton settlement; and the **Town House** *(149 Main St.),* built around 1731 and displaying early school furnishings. They also administer the **East Hampton Town Marine Museum** *(Bluff Rd.)* in Amagansett and the **Boat Shop** *(42 Gann Rd. Daily July-Aug., Sat.-Sun. June and Sept., and by appt.; adm. fee)* at Three Mile Harbor.

Back in East Hampton, visit the **Home Sweet Home Museum** *(14 James Ln. 631-324-0713. Adm. fee),* childhood home of actor, playwright, and diplomat John Howard Payne, who wrote the song by that name. Then check out the **Old Hook Mill** *(N. Main St. 631-324-0713. July-Aug., grounds open year-round; adm. fee),* an 1806 windmill still in working order; it highlights an industry that once flourished on the windy East End. Not far away, **Guild Hall** *(158 Main St. 631-324-0806. Donation),* an art museum, offers changing exhibits by contemporary regional artists as well as lectures, concert series, and films.

Outside the village is the **Pollock-Krasner House and Study Center** *(830 Fireplace Rd. 631-324-4929. By appt.; adm. fee),* the former home and studio of abstract expressionists Jackson Pollock and his wife, Lee Krasner. In addition to documenting Pollock's work, the center stands as a reminder that East Hampton has so many celebrities that it can host an artists vs. writers charity softball game *(Harrick Park. 631-324-8550. Mid-Aug.; donation),* and the **Hamptons International Film Festival** *(631-324-4600. Oct.; adm. fee).* For a dramatic beach walk among dunes and mansions, go south from N.Y. 27 to **Atlantic Avenue Beach** *(631-324-6124. Adm. fee Mem. Day–Labor Day).*

More dune walks lie ahead in **Montauk**★ *(Chamber of Commerce 631-668-2428),* which means "hilly land." Once the home of Montauket Indians, the land passed into the hands of East Hampton colonists in 1686, who moved here to raise cattle. Centuries later, during the 1920s, Montauk figured in developer Carl Fisher's scheme to make the sandy peninsula the Miami Beach of the north. The

plan stalled when the Depression hit, but not before
Fisher marked his territory with the brick Tudor tower
that still stands over the village. Today, Montauk attracts
family vacationers to resorts, motels, and guest houses, its
vast beaches the big lure. Sportfishing charters from the
harbor are also popular, and campers relish the dunes
and beaches at **Hither Hills State Park** *(Off N.Y. 27. 631-
668-2554. Adm. fee Mem. Day–Labor Day),* while golfers enjoy
the Robert Trent Jones course at **Montauk Downs State
Park** *(Off N.Y. 27. 631-668-3781. Adm. fee).*

No place embodies Montauk's dynamic combination
of sound, sand, and sea more than the 724 acres of maritime forest covering the hills of ❹ **Montauk Point State
Park**★★ *(N.Y. 27. 631-668-3781. Adm. fee).* Rocky shores,
cliffs, and woods draw hikers, bikers, and surf anglers.
The **Montauk Point Lighthouse Museum**★ *(End of N.Y.
27. 631-668-2544. June–Columbus Day, phone for winter schedule; adm. fee)* is the focal point here. Not only will exhibits
inform you about the history of this lighthouse dating
from 1796, but you can also climb the spiral staircase to

the top of the 100-
foot tower.

From here you
can see your next
destination, ❺ **Sag
Harbor**★ *(Chamber
of Commerce 631-
725-0011),* about 20
miles to the west.
Arriving via N.Y. 27
and N.Y. 114, you
can tell this is a
thriving yachting
center by the
thicket of masts and
flash of sails. One
of the first two
ports of entry in the
United States, Sag

At the Sag Harbor Whaling Museum

Harbor evolved into a bustling whaling port during the
19th century. Strolling the National Historic District, which
encompasses most of the town, you will see how the
whalers spent their profits, building houses in an extraor-
dinary range of architectural styles. History buffs won't
want to miss the **Sag Harbor Whaling Museum**★ *(100
Main St. 631-725-0770. Mid-May–Sept.; adm. fee),* housed in an
1845 mansion and featuring scrimshaw, ship models, an

Shelter Island ferry

authentic dory, and a menacing collection of harpoons. Then walk next door to the **Customs House** *(631-725-0770. Daily July-Aug., weekends June and Sept.; adm. fee),* which began operation in 1789. It now holds historic documents and period furnishings.

Reach your next port of call via a short ride on the South Ferry *(631-749-1200. Fare)* that plies back and forth across Noyack Bay all day long. Cradled between the arms of the North and South Forks, **Shelter Island**★★ charms walkers and bikers with country roads, miles of water views, a Victorian historic district, and the **Mashomack Nature Preserve**★ *(Off N.Y. 114. 631-749-1001),* covering nearly one-third of the 6,200-acre island. Take time out to birdwatch or hike on the preserve. Or rent a bike at Picozzi's, Inc. *(Deering Harbor Marina. 631-749-0055).* You can also paddle around the island's creeks and harbors with Shelter Island Kayak Tours *(631-749-1990).*

After your exploration of Shelter Island, take the North Ferry *(631-749-0139. Fare)* to **Greenport**★ *(Chamber of Commerce 631-298-5757).* This is a place to linger if you love harbors that exude tradition. Notice the railroad depot as soon as you exit the ferry; it houses the excellent **East End Seaport Maritime Museum**★ *(Foot of Third St. 631-477-2100. Wed.-Mon. June-Sept., Fri.-Sun. May and Oct.; adm. fee).* On view are exhibits about Peconic Bay's fishing industry, the Bug Island Lighthouse restoration, and plans for a shipyard to service tall ships such as the ***Regina Maris*** *(At Claudio's restaurant and pier, Main St. 631-477-0004. June-Sept. Tues., Sat.-Sun.; donation).*

Photographs, artifacts, and memorabilia of the Long

Island Railroad are on view at the **Railroad Museum of Long Island** *(Third and Wiggins Sts. 631-477-0439. Mid-May–mid-Dec. weekends; adm. fee).* (To see rolling stock, you'll have to wait until the drive passes through River-head, where a museum affiliate, located off Griffing Avenue, showcases a steam engine, a rail post office, and a double-decker passenger car.)

Then walk the waterfront and village streets to the oldest marine chandlery in America, **S. T. Preston & Son** *(102 Main St. 631-477-1990),* a good place to shop for seashells, nautical instruments, and ship models. For a short sail on a traditional vessel, board the schooner **Mary E.** *(631-477-8966. Fare).*

Long Island pumpkin patch

If you are in the mood for a picnic, birding, or just a quiet seaside walk, head east to ❻ **Orient Beach State Park**★ *(Main Rd. 631-323-2440. Parking fee Mem. Day–Labor Day),* where miles of penin-sula, beach, and wetlands define the 357 acres of coastal wilderness.

Drive back west on the North Fork for the last leg of this drive, pausing at farmstands before reaching the village of ❼ **Southold.** Here the **Southold Historical Society** *(Main Rd. and Maple Ln. 631-765-5500. July–mid-Sept. Wed., Sat.-Sun.; donation)* main-tains a village complex that revives 18th- and 19th-century rural life on the North Fork. Then visit the **Southold Indian Museum** *(Bayview Rd. 631-765-5577)* to learn about the Native American civilization that pre-ceded the colonists here.

Since the 1970s, winemakers have been discovering that the same microclimate that makes the North Fork great for pota-toes and other vegetables also

Hargrove Winery, Cutchogue

nurtures a variety of wine grapes. More than a dozen wineries now call the area home, and you pass many of them—some offering tours and tastings—on the final few miles of this drive along N.Y. 25. **Pindar Vineyards** *(N.Y. 25, Peconic. 631-734-6200)* is the largest, with vintages ranging from Chardonnay to Merlot.

Hudson River Valley ★

● 200 miles ● 3 days ● Spring and autumn

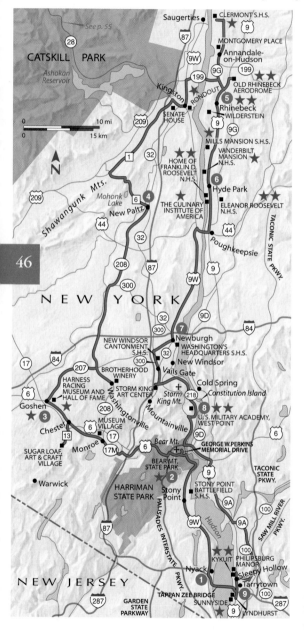

See p. 55

If you look north as you cross the Tappan Zee Bridge (I-287) above the Hudson River, you take in what Dutch explorers saw almost 400 years ago. The river spreads nearly 3 miles wide, carving between mountains and promontories. A glittering path into an emerald land.

You will follow the trails of Indians, adventurers, George Washington's Continental Army, and Gilded Age millionaires, while enjoying vistas that inspired the Hudson River school artists more than a century ago. Sharp peaks, deep valleys, woods, and farms divide artsy, gentrified communities. Historic sites and many of the grandest mansions in America—including FDR's longtime home at Hyde Park—abound.

The drive begins in the funky town of ❶ **Nyack** *(Chamber of Commerce 914-353-2221).* Settled around 1680, this old Dutch farming community now lures city folks seeking weekend refuges. Trendy boutiques, galleries, antique shops, and ethnic restaurants give Nyack something of a Greenwich Village feel. Edward Hopper, the 20th-century painter known for *Nighthawks* and other stark portrayals of loneliness, grew up here. His home, the **Edward Hopper House** *(82 N. Broadway. 914-358-0774. Thurs.-Sun.; donation),* contains materials depicting his life and provides exhibit space for local and national artists.

From Nyack, the drive heads north on US 9W through forest and rolling hills to the town of **Stony Point.** In July 1779, Brig. Gen. "Mad" Anthony Wayne and the Corps of Light Infantry surprised the British garrison here in a nighttime raid that shook British confidence and boosted American morale. **Stony Point Battlefield State Historic Site** *(Off US 9W. 914-786-2521. Mid-April–Oct. Wed.-Sun.)* has guided walking tours, a slide show, military demonstrations, and the remains of British fortifications among the woods and fields near **Stony Point Lighthouse.**

Following US 9W north from the battlefield, you soon find yourself driving alongside forested mountains rising

Bear Mountain Bridge across the Hudson

above the misty Hudson. This route carries you to
❷ **Bear Mountain State Park** ★ *(914-786-5003. Parking fee May–Labor Day),* which shares 54,000 acres with Harriman State Park. Take the George W. Perkins Memorial Drive to the top of 1,305-foot Bear Mountain, where you'll find commanding views of the Hudson River far below. You can see why this site was coveted in the 17th and 18th centuries by French, British, and Americans hoping to control trade on the Hudson. During the Revolutionary War, the Americans commanded two forts here. The

Museum Village, Monroe

park also offers hiking, swimming, golf, boating, cross-country skiing, and camping *(mid-April–mid-Oct.; fee)*. In addition, you will find a wildlife center; a trailside museum; a nature trail; and the Bear Mountain Inn, with rooms and a restaurant.

US 6 and N.Y. 17M lead west to the village of **Monroe,** where the **Museum Village** *(130 Museum Village Rd. 914-782-8247. May-Dec. Wed.-Sun.; adm. fee)* re-creates a pre-industrial, 19th-century village. Most of the 25 buildings—including the blacksmith shop and the print shop—have costumed guides and artisans who demonstrate various crafts. The village hosts a long list of special events, such as sheep shearing and one of the Northeast's largest Civil War encampments.

Now follow N.Y. 17M west and County Rd. 13 (Kings Highway) south among the apple orchards and horse farms of Warwick Valley to **Sugar Loaf, Art & Craft Village** *(Kings Hwy. 914-469-9181)*. This is not a museum, but rather a vital community of more than 50 artists and crafts people, many working in barns and buildings that endure from the 17th century. Over the last 50 years, artists have discovered the charms of Sugar Loaf's rural setting, and have revitalized the village with enterprises ranging from stained-glass artistry to dollmaking. Parking is limited to either end of the village, giving visitors a chance to quietly stroll the wooden sidewalks, shop, catch a gourmet snack, or dive into weekend festivals.

Proceeding west on N.Y. 17M through farm country brings you to ❸ **Goshen**★ *(Chamber of Commerce*

914-294-7741). On a warm summer day, breezes carry the scent of hay and horses, for this prosperous town is the site of the **Goshen Historic Track** *(914-294-5333. Races June-July, call for schedule).* Tucked just off the main street behind historic row houses, the harness racing track looks like a miniature Churchill Downs, with 1890s turrets and wooden bleachers. There are few races these days—and never any betting—but horses and drivers live and train here just as they have since 1838, when harness racing was the common man's sport.

Nearby stands the newly expanded **Harness Racing Museum and Hall of Fame**★ *(240 Main St. 914-294-6330. Scheduled to reopen in fall 1997; adm. fee),* which tells the story of harness racing with state-of-the-art displays.

The drive continues northeast on N.Y. 207 past horse and dairy farms, then south on N.Y. 208 to Washingtonville and the **Brotherhood Winery** *(35 North St. 914-496-9101. Adm. fee),* which claims to be America's oldest winery. Take a tour and sample a variety of vintages ranging from Chablis to cream sherry.

49

Dramatic scenes await farther north on N.Y. 208, which brings you through rolling countryside to the town of ❹ **New Paltz** *(Chamber of Commerce 914-255-0243).* The town's claim to fame is the **Huguenot Street National Historic Landmark District**★★ *(Visitor Center, 6 Broadhead Ave. 914-255-1660. May-Oct. Wed.-Sun.; adm. fee),* a street containing seven house museums (six are original) depicting the lives of upper-middle-class French Protestants who settled here in 1677.

New Paltz gains its vitality today from the student body attending the local state university, as well as from the rock climbers who come to test their skill on **Shawangunks Ridge**★ *(Visitor Center, 301 Mountain Rest Rd., New Paltz. 914-255-0919. Adm. fee).* Also known as "the Gunks," these 300-foot cliffs rate as one of the nation's most popular rock climbing areas. Travelers get a glimpse of them heading northwest out of town on County Rd. 6.

Beyond, you'll see the gate to the **Mohonk Mountain House** *(1000 Mountain Rest Rd./County Rd. 6. 914-255-1000. Day-use fee for hikers).* This 1870s resort hotel on Mohonk Lake looks like a Rhineland castle; it offers hiking, horseback riding, and cross-country skiing, as well as fine accommodations.

Visiting Huguenot Street in New Paltz

A few miles beyond Mohonk, County Rd. 6 joins County Rd. 1, bringing you to the river port of **Kingston,** settled by the Dutch in 1652 and designated New York's first state capital in 1777. Filled with old stone buildings with half-open Dutch doors, the **Stockade District** *(Bounded by N. Front, Clinton, Main, and Green Sts.)* forms the heart of old Kingston. Here, too, you'll find the **Senate House** *(312 Fair St. 914-338-2786. Mid-April–Oct. Wed.-Sun.; adm. fee),* where the New York State Senate first met in 1777. Stop by the Visitor Center of the Kingston Urban Cultural Park *(308 Clinton Ave. 914-331-9506. May-Oct.)* for information and displays on the historic area.

You'll also want to head down to the river and stroll the **Rondout** ★ *(Bounded by Broadway, Abeel, W. Strand, and E. Strand Sts.),* Kingston's 19th-century waterfront district. Here you find boutiques, outdoor cafés, restaurants, a riverside park, boat tours, the **Trolley Museum of New York** *(89 E. Strand. 914-331-3399. Mem. Day–Columbus Day weekends),* and the **Hudson River Maritime Museum** *(1 Rondout Landing. 914-338-0071. May-Oct. Wed.-Mon.; adm. fee).* Another Visitor Center of the Kingston Urban Cultural Park *(20 Broadway. 914-331-7517 or 800-331-1518)* chronicles Kingston's history as a transportation center.

World War I airplane, Old Rhinebeck Aerodrome

Take US 9W north and cross the Hudson on the Kingston-Rhinecliff Bridge *(toll),* into the genteel world of the Gilded Age. At the heart of this world stands the village of ❺ **Rhinebeck** ★★ *(Chamber of Commerce 914-876-4778).* With over 300 sites on the National Register of

Historic Places, the town is a place where high-gloss quaint is an architectural motif. Travelers find themselves drawn to the historic rooms of the 1766 **Beekman Arms** *(4 Mill St. 914-876-7077)*, one of America's oldest continually operating inns; legend says that George Washington slept here.

Vanderbilt Mansion, Hyde Park

Rhinebeck is also home to **Old Rhinebeck Aerodrome**★★ *(Off US 9, N of town. 914-758-8610. Daily May-Oct., air shows Sat.-Sun. mid-June–mid-Oct.; adm. fee)*, where local resident Cole Palen created a World War I–style airdrome to display and fly his collection of vintage aircraft for public entertainment. On summer Saturdays pilots reenact flights from the pioneer aviation era up until the 1930s, while World War I "battles" take place on Sundays.

Rhinebeck lies in the middle of the **Hudson River National Historic Landmark District,** an area recognized for its abundance of historic mansions. North of town, the **Clermont State Historic Site**★ *(Off N.Y. 9G. 518-537-4240. April-Oct. Tues.-Sun.; adm. fee)* was home to seven generations of the politically powerful and socially prominent Livingston family; and **Montgomery Place** *(River Rd., Annandale-on-Hudson. 914-758-5461. April-Oct. Wed.-Mon., Nov.-Dec. weekends; adm. fee)* is a classical revival estate where you can pick your own apples and raspberries in season *(914-758-6338. Fee)*. South of Rhinebeck stands **Wilderstein** *(64 Morton Rd. 914-876-4818. May-Oct. Thurs.-Sun.; adm. fee)*, a fairytale castle on 40 acres. The baronial **Mills Mansion State Historic Site**★ *(Off US 9. 914-889-8851. Mid-April–Oct. Wed.-Sun.; adm. fee)* awaits a few miles farther south. With its 20-leaf dining table, the estate is reputedly one of the settings for novelist Edith Wharton's *The House of Mirth*.

Soon you enter the village of ❻ **Hyde Park** *(Dutchess County Tourism 914-229-0020)*, where architecture buffs will want to stop at the **Vanderbilt Mansion National Historic Site**★ *(Off US 9. 914-229-7770. May-Oct. daily, Nov.-April Wed.-Sun.; adm. fee)*. The 54-room beaux arts palace

Bedroom, Home of Franklin D. Roosevelt
National Historic Site, Hyde Park

was built in 1898 by Frederick Vanderbilt, grandson of railroad magnate Cornelius Vanderbilt. Once called "the finest place on the Hudson between New York and Albany," the estate is nothing short of a monument to the wealth that made the Vanderbilts America's richest family in the 19th century.

Less grand, but carrying the weight of history, is another Hyde Park estate, the **Home of Franklin D. Roosevelt National Historic Site**★★ *(US 9. 914-229-2501. Wed.-Sun.; adm. fee).* Franklin Delano Roosevelt grew up in this Georgian colonial house, part of the family estate known as Springwood. During Roosevelt's long Presidency, when he entertained the likes of Winston Churchill and other heads of state, it became known as the "summer White House." Visitors will see not only Roosevelt memorabilia and the presidential library, but also the furnishings and possessions of the President's mother, Sara, who stamped the place with her strong personality.

Never totally comfortable living in her mother-in-law's house, Eleanor built her own retreat a few miles away and called it Val-Kill, now the **Eleanor Roosevelt**

U.S. Military Academy bandstand overlooking the Hudson at West Point

National Historic Site ★★ *(N.Y. 9G. 914-229-9422. May–Oct. Wed.–Sun.; adm. fee).* During the Depression, the "First Lady of the World" operated a furniture factory here, employing farm youths and crafts people to build Early American reproductions. In her later years, Eleanor lived at Val-Kill, regularly receiving world leaders.

A final stop in the Hyde Park area is the **Culinary Institute of America**★ *(US 9. 914-452-9600 or 914-471-6608. Closed Sun. and two weeks in July and Dec.).* This one-time Jesuit seminary is now the setting for one of America's premier cooking schools. The courtyard and hallways buzz with students in their white chef hats—and the whole place smells like heaven. You can eat in four different restaurants (regional American, French, Italian, and contemporary), but call well in advance for reservations, and ask about the dress code.

Escape traffic by following US 44 across the river at Poughkeepsie. From here, head to the Newburgh area on US 9W to see where George Washington and his Continental Army waited out peace negotiations with the British at the close of the Revolutionary War. Washington stationed himself and his staff for 16½ months in **7** **Newburgh,** at the Hasbrouck House—now called **Washington's Headquarters State Historic Site** *(84 Liberty St. 914-562-1195. Mid-April–mid-Oct. Wed.–Sun.; adm. fee).* The site features a museum that chronicles the Revolutionary War from 1782 to 1783, as well as the restored house full of period reproductions. Washington's 7,000 soldiers camped out in nearby New Windsor, at the **New Windsor Cantonment State Historic Site** *(N.Y. 300. 914-561-1765. Wed.–Sun.; adm. fee).* A shady trail winds past reconstructed campsites, and costumed soldiers demonstrate musketry, blacksmithing, and open-fire cookery.

If modern art captures your imagination, don't miss the **Storm King Art Center** *(Off N.Y. 32 on Old Pleasant Hill Rd., Mountainville. 914-534-3115. April–Nov.; adm. fee),* south on N.Y. 32. Here, 120 sculptures by renowned artists including Alexander Calder stand out against the mountains.

Pick up N.Y. 218 (Old Storm King Highway), which offers heart-stopping vistas as it twists around Storm King Mountain on the edge of cliffs high above the Hudson. This route carries you through the **8** **United States Military Academy, West Point**★★ *(914-938-2638).* The best way to see the large, historic post—a virtual town—is to take a one-hour bus tour *(fee)* from the **Visitor Center** *(Bldg. 2107, Main St. near Thayer Gate).* If you have time, you might attend one of the free cadet concerts

Treason at West Point

Nicknamed West Point for its geographic location, the site has been garrisoned since 1778, when colonists began to construct a series of fortifications to prevent the British from controlling the Hudson River. However, West Point's greatest threat came from within. In 1780 Brig. Gen. Benedict Arnold—hero of Saratoga, the turning point in the Revolution—served as commandant of the site. For many reasons, Arnold became disenchanted with the colonists and made overtures to the British. He provided the plans of West Point to a British agent for £20,000, but the agent was captured before returning to British lines. Arnold escaped and went on to lead British forces in Connecticut and Virginia. He ultimately died in obscurity in England.

Gravesite of Gen. Daniel Delavan at Sleepy Hollow Cemetery

Cold Spring

Across the Hudson from Storm King Mountain and West Point lies the village of **Cold Spring** *(Chamber of Commerce 914-265-9060)*, one of those towns that defies this century and the next. Sloping downhill to the bandstand gazebo by the river, Main Street is a row of polished 19th-century facades. Shopping here means searching for something old, not something new. A host of antique dealers fill their shops with everything from vintage clothing to country crockery and handmade dolls. Here you can browse a used book emporium, brunch at the old steamboat wharf, sup in the restored train station, and pick your bed from a collection of B&Bs with period furnishings. Even the hounds sleeping among the roots of the shade trees look like they've been killing time for a hundred years. City folk love it.

54

performed on summer evenings, or take the ferry to explore **Constitution Island** *(914-446-8676. Mid-June–mid-Sept. Wed.-Thurs.; fare. Reservations recommended)*, dotted with the ruins of Revolutionary War fortifications.

Exiting the academy to the south, cross the river and go south on N.Y. 9D for a few miles of cliff-hanging Hudson vistas. To avoid traffic, follow US 9, N.Y. 9A, and N.Y. 100 to **Sleepy Hollow** (formerly North Tarrytown). Here awaits **Philipsburg Manor** *(US 9. 914-631-3992. Wed.-Mon. mid-April–Dec., Sat.-Sun. in March; adm. fee)*, an early 18th-century working farm. A shuttle leaves from here for **Kykuit**★★ *(914-631-9491. Mid-April–Oct. Wed.-Mon.; adm. fee. Reservations required)*, the country home of several generations of Rockefellers, and the crown jewel of the Hudson Valley mansions.

Sleepy Hollow Cemetery *(540 N. Broadway. 914-631-0085)* is the final resting place of Washington Irving and other notables. Next door, the **Old Dutch Church of Sleepy Hollow** *(914-631-1123. Tours Mem. Day–Labor Day on Sun.)* was said to be the haunt of a headless Hessian ghost—giving birth to Irving's *The Legend of Sleepy Hollow*.

The drive ends in ❾ **Tarrytown**, site of **Lyndhurst** *(635 S. Broadway/US 9. 914-631-4481. Mid-April–Oct. Tues.-Sun.; adm. fee)*, an 1838 Gothic Revival mansion loaded with original furniture and art. Finally, dreamers and literary fans will want to tour Washington Irving's **Sunnyside**★ *(Off US 9. 914-591-8763. Daily April-Dec., Sat.-Sun. in March; adm. fee)*, where the author lived off and on from 1835 until his death in 1859. Costumed guides lead you through this architectural flight of fancy, which Irving once referred to as being as "full of angles and corners as an old cocked hat."

Albany and the Catskills ★

● **300 miles** ● **3 days** ● **Spring and autumn**

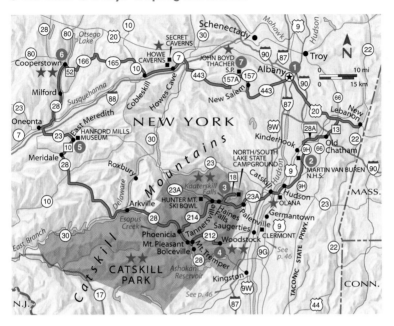

See p. 46

Nowhere in New York is such a contrast between dynamism and serenity more obvious than in the Albany-Catskill region. The tour starts with a walk through the capital city, where historic buildings such as the New York State Capitol face off with the ultra-modern "Egg." The drive heads southeast into the countryside to view the contrasting simplicity of Shaker life and the grandeur of a Hudson River estate before curving west across the river. Entering the Catskills, the route weaves among

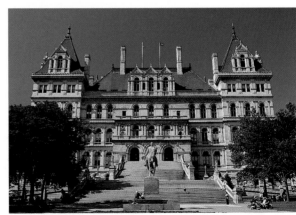

State Capitol, Albany

3,500-foot peaks, fishing streams, and trailheads, pausing at the artist colony of Woodstock.

More contrasts emerge as you head north to Coopers-town, where the National Baseball Hall of Fame and the Fenimore House Museum keep company. Finally, spectacular caves and a hiking trail break up the serenity of backroad touring through dairy country.

In the Shaker Museum, Old Chatham

Begin in ❶ **Albany** at the **Albany Visitor Center** *(25 Quackenbush Sq. 518-434-5132),* just off the downtown exit of I-787. Exhibits describe the history of the region, which Henry Hudson first visited in 1609 while searching for a passage to the Far East. Lying near the head of the navigable part of the Hudson River, Albany prospered under Dutch, then English, then American rule as a transportation, industrial, and political center. The Visitor Center offers walking tour maps of the city's several historic districts.

In the center of town looms the French Renaissance **New York State Capitol** *(State St. 518-474-2418. Call for schedule),* built from 1867 to 1898 and now anchoring the eastern edge of Empire State Plaza. Thousands of stone carvings of faces—some of historic figures—adorn walls and pillars throughout the building. But no carvings are as compelling as those found on the Million Dollar Staircase, which took 13 years to complete. You can tour the Senate and Assembly chambers, as well as the ceremonial office, once used by Theodore Roosevelt, Franklin Delano Roosevelt, and Nelson Rockefeller.

American Museum of Firefighting, Hudson

Now stroll through **Nelson A. Rockefeller Empire State Plaza** *(Bounded by Swan, Madison, State, and Eagle Sts. 518-474-2418),* which cost a billion dollars and was the fulfillment of Nelson Rockefeller's dream to revitalize downtown. Catch a concert at the egg-shaped **Performing Arts Center** *(Mid-plaza. 518-473-1845),* and ride the elevator up to the Tower Building observation deck for sweeping city views. At the plaza's other end, you'll find the **New York State Museum** *(518-474-5877),* one of the nation's oldest state museums. Exhibits focus on the Adirondack wilderness and New York City.

The nearby **Albany Institute of History and Art** *(125 Washington Ave. 518-463-4478. Wed.-Sun.; adm. fee)* displays paintings, artifacts, and decorative arts representing life in the upper Hudson Valley from European settlement to the present.

From the institute, head south on Dove Street to **Robinson Square** on Hamilton Street to explore a neighborhood of 19th-century brownstone row houses reclaimed by gentrification and alive with shops and restaurants. From here, it's just a one block stroll west to **Lark Street,** Albany's "Little Greenwich Village," featuring Sunday art shows in summer.

Historic house mavens will want to stop at three of Albany's most famous residences. Built in 1798, the federal-style **Ten Broeck Mansion** *(9 Ten Broeck Pl. 518-436-9826. Mid-May–mid-Dec. Thurs.-Sun.; adm. fee)* belonged to Abraham Ten Broeck, a Revolutionary War patriot. Another patriot, Philip Schuyler, lived at the 1761 **Schuyler Mansion State Historic Site** *(32 Catherine St. 518-434-0834. Mid-April–Oct., and by appt.; adm. fee);* George Washington, Benjamin Franklin, and Benedict Arnold all visited here. **Historic Cherry Hill** *(523½ S. Pearl St. 518-434-4791. Closed Mon. and Jan.; adm. fee),* completed in 1787 by Philip van Rensselaer, has decorative arts and personal possessions depicting the lives of five van Rensselaer generations.

In the late 1800s, a group of English men and women called Shakers immigrated to the Albany area to freely practice their communal religion. To explore an early set-

tlement, drive southeast of Albany on US 20 to **New Lebanon** and the **Mt. Lebanon Shaker Village** ★ *(Darrow Rd., at the Darrow School. 518-794-9500. June-Aug. daily, fall weekends; adm. fee).* Tours visit a meetinghouse and other restored buildings. A short country drive away in Old Chatham, the **Shaker Museum and Library** *(88 Shaker Museum Rd., off County Rd. 13.*

Artist Frederic Edwin Church's home, Olana

518-794-9100. May-Oct. Wed.-Mon.; adm. fee) displays a fine collection of functionally elegant furniture—the by-product of the strong work ethic and imagination that characterized the Shakers' communal lifestyle.

By contrast, Martin van Buren, the nation's eighth President, celebrated his individualism and self-made prosperity at his retirement estate, Lindenwald—now the ❷ **Martin van Buren National Historic Site** *(518-758-9689. May-Oct. daily, Nov. weekends.; adm. fee).* Visiting Lindenwald, located just south of Kinderhook on N.Y. 9H, offers insights into the forces behind the astute politician, who formed the coalition that became the modern Democratic party.

Take N.Y. 9H south and N.Y. 66 west to **Hudson,** where you will discover the nation's largest collection of fire-fighting apparatus and memorabilia at the **American Museum of Firefighting** *(125 Harry Howard Ave. 518-828-7695).* A highlight is the 1731 Nesham Engine, the first fire truck used in New York City.

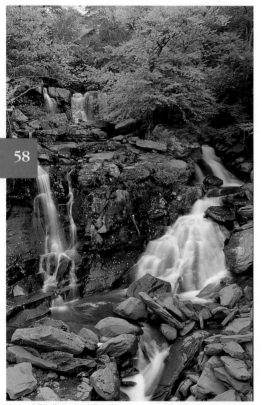

58

South of town lies **Olana**★ *(N.Y. 9G/N.Y. 23B. 518-828-0135. April-Oct. Wed.-Sun.; adm. fee),* the fanciful estate of one of the most celebrated Hudson River school painters. After his 1857 painting of Niagara Falls won him world recognition and fortune, Frederic Edwin Church designed this 16-room Persian-Italianate castle and filled it with his own work and objets d'art collected abroad.

The inspiration of many of the Hudson River school painters lies 15 miles west, across the Hudson River, in the Catskill Mountains. From the town of Catskill, go south on US 9W and west on N.Y. 23A into **Catskill Park**★★, 705,280 acres of tightly packed mountains and deep valleys. Vast tracts of public land totaling 287,100 acres constitute the **Catskill Forest Preserve** *(607-652-7365),* which must be "forever kept as wild" in accordance with 1885 legislation.

Kaaterskill Falls in Catskill Park

Ahead you pass through the area inhabited by Rip Van Winkle in Washington Irving's *The Legend of Sleepy Hollow.* The road twists toward mountain summits, passing **Bastion Falls**★. To visit ❸ **Kaaterskill Falls**★★, a favorite setting for Hudson River school artists, proceed to the junction of N.Y. 23A and Kaaterskill Creek, near the village of Haines Falls. Leaving from the highway's north side, the easy Kaaterskill Falls Trail brings you to the base of the two-tiered falls.

For one of the best views in the Catskills, take County Rd. 18 north from Haines Falls to the North/South Lake

State Campground *(518-584-5058. May–mid-Oct.; adm. fee)*. Park at the beach parking lot at North Lake, and look for a path leading uphill. In five minutes, you'll reach the former site of the **Catskill Mountain House.** The Greek Revival resort is long gone, but the fabulous **view**★★ still peers 2,000 feet down into the valley.

Back on N.Y. 23A, continue west through the mountains, passing Tannersville to the **Hunter Mountain Ski Bowl** *(518-263-4223. Ski season Nov.-April; fee),* with a 1,600-foot vertical drop. More than 50 trails make this one of New York's most developed ski areas.

N.Y. 214 carries travelers south to **Phoenicia,** where outfitters offer inner tubes, safety equipment, and shuttle service for tube trips down Esopus Creek. **Town Tinker Tube Rental** *(10 Bridge St. 914-688-5553. Mid-May–mid-Sept.)* is the oldest operation here. After tubing down the river, consider returning to Phoenicia aboard the **Catskill Mountain Railroad** *(N.Y. 28, Mt. Pleasant. 914-688-7400. Late May–mid-Oct. weekends; fare).* The **Empire State Railway Museum** *(High St. 914-688-7501. Mem. Day–Labor Day Sat.-Sun.; donation),* located in the 1899 village station, offers exhibits on railroad history in New York and the Catskills.

The drive continues south on N.Y. 28 and east on N.Y. 212. You know you're getting close to the famous art colony in Woodstock when you come face to face with a set of celestial eyes painted on a barn silo. Peek inside to see the "world's largest kaleidoscope" at **Catskill Corners**★ *(N.Y. 28, Mt. Tremper. 914-688-7335. Adm. fee.).* In a dozen dizzy minutes, the kaleidoscope will blast you with a psychedelic image show depicting 300 years of American history accompanied by surround sound.

When you roll into ❹ **Woodstock**★★ *(Chamber of Commerce 914-679-6234),* hippie folk with tie-dye shirts, long hair, beads, sandals, and granny dresses will hark you back to the sixties. Young musicians gather in the small park at the center of town in front of the tidy white church…just as Joan Baez and Bob Dylan did over 30 years ago. While the legendary 1969 rock concert didn't happen here (it took place 50 miles away in Bethel), Woodstock's mystique as a place of magic and inspiration for the young—and young at heart—endures. The mountain setting, 19th-century architecture, hippie boutiques, trendy restaurants, and artsy citizens have a way of making even the most jaded travelers pause to listen to the music and sniff the incense in the air.

Woodstock is a good base for exploring the trails, peaks, and backroads of the Catskills, as well as for

59

Woodstock color

Guru of Nature Writers

When the Industrial Revolution and its promise of wealth all but overwhelmed the American psyche at the opening of the 20th century, one voice spoke out eloquently in favor of appreciation and preservation of the national wilderness—John Burroughs. His zeal, essays, poems, and books (including *Locusts and Wild Honey*) caught the attention of Teddy Roosevelt, Henry Ford, and other titans, and engendered an environmental conscience. Burroughs drew his inspiration from a vista in the Catskills. You can see his thinking spot, "Boyhood Rock," his studio, and his grave at **John Burroughs Memorial Field** *(N.Y. 30, N of Roxbury)*. The view here is dramatic, the solitude profound.

stocking up for fishing, hiking, mountain-biking, and skiing adventures. There are a lot of B&Bs in the area; one uncommon lodging is **Onteora, The Mountain House** *(96 Piney Point Rd., Boiceville. 914-657-6233)*. The former retreat of Richard Hellman the mayonnaise magnate offers a high-mountain view of sunsets over purple peaks.

Backtrack to N.Y. 28 and meander northwest to **Arkville,** the hub for the **Delaware and Ulster Rail Ride** *(Arkville Depot. 914-586-DURR or 800-225-4132. Weekends Mem. Day–June and Sept.-Oct., Wed.-Sun. July-Aug.; fare)*. Hop aboard a restored car and wind through a mountain landscape. The route continues northwest on N.Y. 28, then east at Meridale on County Rd. 10 to the well-scrubbed village of **East Meredith.** Here, a mill pond and waterwheel drive the ❺ **Hanford Mills Museum** *(County Rd. 12. 607-278-5744. May-Oct., call for hours; adm. fee)*, whose interior you tour on walkways. Interpreters grind grain and use water-driven woodworking machinery to craft barrel lids just as was done a century ago. Leave town on N.Y. 23 and rejoin N.Y. 28 as it curls farther north through dairy country. In **Milford,** car buffs will find 35 Chevy sports cars linked to popular culture at the **Corvette Hall of Fame** *(N.Y. 28. 607-547-4135. Late Feb.-Dec.; adm. fee)*.

Then head into the major tourist attraction and enclave of nostalgia— ❻ **Cooperstown** ★★ *(Chamber of Commerce 607-547-9983)*. Once a quiet retreat on Otsego Lake, this town of large 19th-century houses and gift shops has become a mecca for young children and their parents intent on visiting the **National Baseball Hall of Fame and Museum** ★★ *(Main St. 607-547-7200. Adm. fee)*. The sports shrine is packed with three floors of memorabilia, including photographs, clothing, equipment, carved wooden statues of baseball stars, and Babe Ruth's locker.

Since Cooperstown traffic can be daunting on summer weekends and parking is limited, you might wish to leave your car at one of the marked lots at the edge of town and take the **Cooperstown Trolley** *(607-547-2411. Daily mid-June–Labor Day, weekends late May–mid-June and Labor Day–mid-Oct.; fare)* to the Hall of Fame. The trolley will also drop you off at the **Farmer's Museum and Village Crossroads** *(Lake Rd. 607-547-1450. Tues.-Sun. in April, daily May-Oct., Tues.-Sat. in Nov., Fri.-Sun. in Dec.; adm. fee)*.

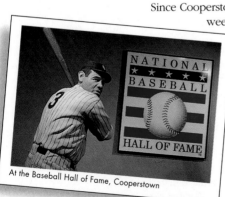

At the Baseball Hall of Fame, Cooperstown

Cooperstown area farmstead

This country village re-creation portrays rural life in the region a century ago. In one of the antique-filled historical buildings you'll find the Cardiff Giant, a gypsum statue that was a famous 19th-century hoax. Across the street, the **Fenimore House Museum** *(607-547-1400. Tues.-Sun. in April, daily May-Oct., Tues.-Sat. in Nov., Fri.-Sun. in Dec.; adm. fee)* displays 700 pieces of Native American art. The museum is located on the former cabin site of favorite native son James Fenimore Cooper, the author of *The Last of the Mohicans.*

The drive back to Albany provides a traffic-free meander through Appalachian foothills dotted with orchards and dairy farms. An hour east of Cooperstown, you hit a region where water has eroded limestone into extensive caverns and dramatic escarpments. **Howe Caverns**★ *(Off N.Y. 7, Howes Cave. 518-296-8900. Adm. fee)* and **Secret Caverns** *(Off N.Y. 7. 518-296-8558. April-Nov.; adm. fee)* both offer guided tours through domed grottoes laced with underground streams, falls, and—at Howe—a boat tour on an underground lake. Near the caves stands the **Iroquois Indian Museum** *(Caverns Rd., Howes Cave. 518-296-8949. April-Dec.; adm. fee),* whose seasonal festivals *(fee)* add vitality to its collection of art, artifacts, and crafts.

Just before Albany's suburbs, stop at ➐ **John Boyd Thacher State Park**★ *(N.Y. 157, New Salem. 518-872-1237. Mem. Day–Labor Day; adm. fee).* Here, the 0.5-mile **Indian Ladder Geological Trail**★ climbs atop an escarpment overlooking pine barrens that cover the seafloor of an ancient ocean.

Adirondacks ★★

● **450 miles** ● **4 to 5 days** ● **Spring through autumn**

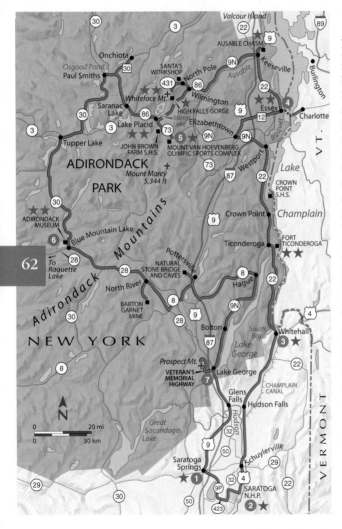

To travel the Adirondack and North Country region is to travel back to other times. Beginning with the medicinal baths, fashionable shops, and thoroughbred racing of Saratoga Springs, the route then heads north, stopping at historic battle sites. Turning west into the Adirondack Mountains, it explores America's largest state park, 6-million-acre Adirondack Park. Trout streams and 4,000-foot peaks mark the trail to Lake Placid, site of two Winter Olympics. Farther west, mountains are replaced by the forests and lakes of the Adirondack State Forest Preserve, home of the extensive Adirondack Museum and the "great camps" of the country's super-wealthy in the 19th century. The trip ends with a drive south along Lake George, described by Thomas Jefferson as "the most beautiful water I ever saw."

Bubbling mineral springs suitable for drinking and bathing have made ❶ **Saratoga Springs**★ an oasis for centuries. You can drink the salubrious waters from fountains in 33-acre **Congress Park**★ at the center of town, right across the street from the **Visitor Center** (*Saratoga Springs Urban Cultural Park, 297 Broadway. 518-587-3241. April-Nov. daily, Dec.-March Mon.-Sat.*), which has information on several self-guided walking tours. Within the park, the Italianate **Canfield Casino**★ *(518-584-6920. June-Sept. daily, Oct.-May Wed.-Sun.; adm. fee),* a one-time gambling emporium, contains two museums tracing the town's evolution from village to famous spa.

Just east of the park sits the **Saratoga Race Course**★ *(Union Ave. 518-584-6200. Late July–Aug.; adm. fee),* built during the Civil War and host to the country's oldest

Horse and jockey at Saratoga Race Course

stakes racing event, the Travers Cup. August is racing month, when the track fills with ladies in broad-brimmed hats, gentlemen with optimistic smiles, and beautiful horses. After the races, stroll across the street to the **National Museum of Racing and Hall of Fame** *(191 Union Ave. 518-584-0400. Adm. fee),* or descend upon the town's shops, cafés, and restaurants. Then head southwest on N.Y. 50 to **Saratoga Spa State Park**★ *(518-584-2535. Parking fee in summer),* where two different spas offer mineral

Revolutionary War fife and drum corps, Fort Ticonderoga

baths in private tubs. Also in the park, the **Saratoga Performing Arts Center**★ *(518-584-9330. June-Aug.; fee for shows)* offers outdoor performances by the New York City Ballet, the New York City Opera, and the Philadelphia Symphony Orchestra, all of which summer here.

If you have more than a day to spend in town, consider a visit to the **National Museum of Dance** *(98 S. Broadway. 518-584-2225. Mem. Day–early Dec. Tues.-Sun.; adm. fee),* where a hall of fame honors American dancers, and you can watch dance rehearsals. Then don your thinking cap and take a stroll in the rose gardens at the **Yaddo** artist colony *(Union Ave. 518-584-0746),* where gifted artists gather, or among the academics of nearby **Skidmore College** *(815 N. Broadway. 518-584-5000).*

Travel southeast on N.Y. 9P along Saratoga Lake to N.Y. 423. Approaching the Hudson River, you pass through battlefields of the American Revolution. This history is preserved at ❷ **Saratoga National Historic Park**★ *(N.Y. 32. 518-664-9821. Adm. fee May-Oct.),* where in October 1777, American Revolutionaries, including Benedict Arnold, defeated 9,000 redcoats under Gen. John Burgoyne in the Battle of Saratoga. Artifacts and a short film at the Visitor Center explain this turning point in the Revolutionary War that caused the French to side with the Rebels. Maps highlight the military events along this stretch of the Hudson River.

The battle took place near **Schuylerville,** originally named Saratoga and renamed to honor Gen. Philip Schuyler. His reconstructed summer house—now the **Gen. Philip Schuyler House** *(S of Schuylerville on US 4. 518-664-9821. Summer only; adm. fee)*—was restored a month after burning in the battle. While in town, check out the views from the 155-foot-high granite **Saratoga Battle Monument.** Begun in 1887 atop the hill that was site of Burgoyne's last encampment, its base displays three statues of famous Revolutionary War leaders. The fourth niche, planned for Benedict Arnold, remains empty.

Less than an hour's drive north lies the town of ❸ **Whitehall**★ *(Chamber of Commerce 518-499-2292),* self-proclaimed birthplace of the U.S. Navy. Here, at Lake Champlain's extreme southern end, Benedict Arnold assembled a flotilla to fight the British fleet at Valcour Island. Though trounced by the British in October 1776, Arnold kept his enemy from moving south for a year. To learn more about Arnold's "navy," the battle, and Whitehall's shipyards, stop by the **Skenesborough Museum** *(US 4. 518-499-0716. Mid-June–Labor Day daily, Labor Day–mid-Oct. weekends, and by appt.; adm. fee),* where wooden models of the early ships are displayed. Outside lies the hull of the **USS *Ticonderoga,*** raised from Lake Champlain after being sunk in the War of 1812. You can also pick up self-guided walking tour pamphlets for the town here.

Cruising the Camps

To get a taste of the lavish summer lifestyles of the Adirondacks' elite in the 19th century, head west from Blue Mountain Lake along N.Y. 28 to **Raquette Lake,** where many of the "great camps" were built. Here you can visit **Great Camp Sagamore** *(Off N.Y. 28. 315-354-5311. Tours July–Labor Day daily, Labor Day–Columbus Day Sat.-Sun.; adm. fee)* and learn how Alfred Vanderbilt assembled this self-sufficient village to provide a few weeks of "rusticating" for his family every year. Or hop aboard the classic lake steamer, the **W.W. Durant** *(Off N.Y. 28. 315-354-5532. July-Aug. daily, Sat.-Sun. mid-May–June and Sept.–mid-Oct.; fare),* and cruise the shores.

Continuing north on N.Y. 22 across South Bay, in 20 miles you see the stone ramparts of **Fort Ticonderoga**★★ *(N.Y. 74, off N.Y. 22. 518-585-2821. May-Oct.; adm. fee)* rising on a point where Lake Champlain pinches to the width of

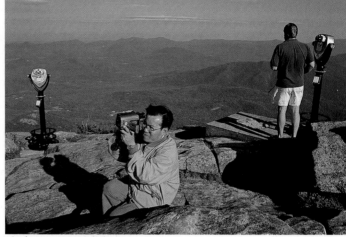

Whiteface Mountain overlook

a modest river. Built by the French in 1755 and restored to this era, the fort contains a museum, a blockhouse, and barracks. Here history crackles with fired cannons and uniformed interpreters, who march and drill to the fife and drum. The museum collection illustrates how the British won the fort during the French and Indian War after a battle that cost almost 2,000 men...and how Ethan Allen and the Green Mountain Boys wrenched the fort from the British after a surprise attack in 1775.

Fifteen miles north lies another lakeside, French-built fort where first the British, and then the Green Mountain Boys, prevailed. **Crown Point State Historic Site** *(Bridge Rd. 518-597-3666. May-Oct. Wed.-Sun.; adm. fee)* presents haunting ruins of both French and British forts, including barracks, stonework, and the remains of a dry moat. The park also offers a Visitor Center and a serene lakeshore.

Follow Lake Champlain's western shore past trim summer houses to the hamlet of **Westport,** alive with art studios, yachting, and summer stock at the **Depot Theatre** *(Pleasant St./N.Y. 9. 518-962-4449. Late May–mid-Sept.).* Veering west on N.Y. 9N, travelers see the sky fill with the highest peaks of the Adirondack Mountains, including 5,344-foot Mount Marcy. Within the Boquet River Valley lies **Elizabethtown** and the **Adirondack History Center**★ *(US 9. 518-873-6466. Mid-May–mid-Oct.; adm. fee).* Here a formal garden, light-and-sound show, and displays illustrate life in the mountains and the Champlain Valley.

Before you get caught up in these big mountains, go north on US 9 and head back to the lakeshore on County Rd. 12 for a visit to ❹ **Essex**★★ *(Essex Community*

View from the Olympic ski jump, Lake Placid

Indian Museum artwork, Onchiota

Heritage Organization 518-963-7088). An impressive ensemble of pre-Civil War architecture, the entire town is on the National Register of Historic Places. Take time to walk the streets, stroll the once-booming waterfront, and ride the **Lake Champlain Ferry** *(802-864-9804. April-Dec.; fare)* for a scenic, 20-minute trip to Charlotte, Vermont.

Open to the public since 1870, **Ausable Chasm**★ *(2144 US 9, N of Keeseville. 518-834-7454. Mem. Day–Columbus Day; adm. fee)* introduces travelers to the roiling Ausable River, which formed the deep sandstone fissure. Featured are a walking trail and raft rides.

N.Y. 9N and N.Y. 86 carry you southwest along the Ausable River into high valleys, where 4,867-foot **Whiteface Mountain**★★ looms above the town of **Wilmington** and a variety of attractions. Families gravitate to **Santa's Workshop** *(N.Y. 431, North Pole. 518-946-2211. June–early Oct.)*, a Christmas theme park with live reindeer, shops, and storybook characters. Motorists overlook both Vermont and Canada from the **Whiteface Mountain Veterans' Memorial Highway (N.Y. 431)**★ *(518-946-7175. Mid-May–mid-Oct.; toll)*, which climbs 8 miles to the summit. With a 3,216-foot vertical drop—the largest drop of any ski area in the East—the **Whiteface Mountain Chairlift Skyride** *(N.Y. 86, 7 miles N of Lake Placid. 518-523-1655 or*

800-462-623. Fare) offers another way to see the views relished by Olympians. *adm. fee).* And hikers walk along **High Falls Gorge**★ *(N.Y. 86, 4.5 miles W of Wilmington. 518-946-2278. June-Aug.; adm. fee)* to view falls and rapids.

Travelers looking for lodging, restaurants, culture, and excitement will take a time-out at **Lake Placid**★★, south on N.Y. 86, which pulses with sports in every season. Both the 1932 and 1980 Winter Olympics were held here, and the town remains a favorite training ground for world-class athletes. Start at the Visitor Center at **Olympic Center**★ *(24 Main St. 518-523-1655 or 800-447-5224)* to get oriented, find lodging, and peruse a long list of ongoing special events, ranging from year-round ski jumping and ice dancing to horse shows and concerts. You can also gather material on recreational opportunities before touring the center's four ice rinks, where the hockey teams, speed skaters, and figure-skating stars train.

South of town watch the competition or enjoy the 26-story view from the ski-jumping tower at the 120-meter **Olympic Jumping Complex**★★ *(N.Y. 73. 518-523-1655. Adm. fee).* For a historical aside, stop by the **John Brown Farm State Historic Site** *(John Brown Rd., off N.Y. 73. 518-523-3900. Late May–Oct. Wed.-Sun., grounds open year-round)* to the see the restored homestead and grave of the famed abolitionist. The wild at heart should continue south on N.Y. 73 to the ❺ **Mount Van Hoevenberg Olympic Sports Complex**★ *(N.Y. 73. 518-523-4436. Closed Mon. Dec.-March; adm. fee),* to ride a luge *(winter only)* or shoot the curves of the bobsled run (using wheeled sleds in warm weather), with a professional driver and brakeman.

For more than a century, travelers have found refuge from the frenzied world at **Saranac Lake,** 10 miles west of Lake Placid. Four U.S. Presidents—Coolidge, McKinley, Theodore Roosevelt,

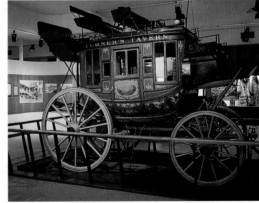

Horse coach, Adirondack Museum

and Harrison—along with Mark Twain, Albert Einstein, and many others flocked to Saranac's sanatoriums, "cure" cottages, and hotels to breathe the lake's crisp air in hopes of staving off tuberculosis. Since the advent of a pharmaceutical cure for tuberculosis in the 1950s, Saranac Lake has evolved into a low-key resort town where vacationing families come for weeks, months, or seasons.

Camp Sagamore cabin, Raquette Lake

Hyde Collection ★

Just beyond the neon signs of Lake George, in a corner of the 19th-century mill town of **Glens Falls,** stands a Florentine-Renaissance villa housing the **Hyde Collection** *(161 Warren St. 518-792-1761. Jan.-April Wed.-Sun., May-Dec. Tues.-Sun.; adm. fee).* The house, furnishings, and art collection are the legacies of Louis and Charlotte Pruyn Hyde, who built a fortune from such Adirondack resources as lumber and waterways. Exhibits, which change regularly, include paintings from the last four centuries of Western art—Leonardo to Picasso—including Cézanne's *Trees* and Winslow Homer's A *Good One, Adirondacks.*

For a tour map to the town's historic cottages, spas, and inns, stop at the **Visitor Center** *(Chamber of Commerce, 30 Main St. 518-891-1990).* The staff can direct you to the **Robert Louis Stevenson Cottage** *(Stevenson Ln. 518-891-1990. July–mid-Sept. Tues.-Sun.; adm. fee),* where memorabilia highlights the author's life at Saranac. He came for "the cure" during the winter of 1887-88.

A fifteen-minute drive north and east on N.Y. 3, Oregon Plains Road, and County Rd. 30 brings you to the **Six Nations Indian Museum** *(County Rd. 30, Onchiota. 518-891-2299. July-Aug.; adm. fee),* where displays highlight Iroquois confederacy life in the Adirondacks before and during colonial times. Head west to the town of **Paul Smiths,** where a classic example of a patrician "great camp" awaits at **White Pine Camp** *(White Pine Rd., off N.Y. 86. 518-327-3030. Mem. Day–Columbus Day, and by appt.; adm. fee).* Twenty buildings are open for tour, plus 2 miles of trails. One visits an elegant Japanese teahouse on an island.

N.Y. 30 winds south into the wilder reaches of the Adirondacks, where the mountains recede and the road curls through pine forest. To get a thorough, and thoroughly enjoyable, sense of backcountry life, stop at the ❻ **Adirondack Museum ★★** *(N.Y. 30, Blue Mountain Lake. 518-352-7311. Mid-May–mid-Oct.; adm. fee).* With 22 exhibits, plus video and audio displays and live demonstrations, the museum draws visitors into the world of lumberjacks, miners, trappers, steamboaters, railroaders, and the wealthy whose elaborate camps they serviced. There's even a locomotive with a private rail car.

Heading toward Lake George via N.Y. 28, N.Y. 8, and US 9, there are two stops for the rock hound—**Barton Garnet Mine Tours** *(Barton Mines Rd., off N.Y. 28 in North*

River. 518-251-2706. Mid-May–Aug.; adm. fee) and the **Natural Stone Bridge and Caves** *(Stonebridge Rd., off US 9 in Pottersville. 518-494-2283. June–early Oct.; adm. fee)*, with geodes and other stones on display and for sale.

After rejoining N.Y. 8, wander east to **Lake George** and follow the shore south to get a clear sense of what North Country folk mean when they say the Adirondacks are endangered. Along the outskirts of the town of ❼ **Lake George,** a carnival atmosphere replaces the serene wilderness. While these lands are in Adirondack Park, no law prohibits the development of private property, amusement parks, motels, and mini-golf courses.

You can try and gain space aboard one of the classic boats of the **Lake George Steamship Co.**★ *(Steel Pier on Beach Rd. 518-668-5777. Call for schedule; fare)* for a sunset cruise and watch as the water, mountains, and forest dwarf the mansions of **Millionaires' Row.** Or take the **Veteran's Memorial Highway** *(Off US 9, Lake George. 518-668-3352. Mid-May–Oct.; adm. fee)* to the top of Prospect Mountain. But you must wonder at the symbolism of **Fort William Henry** *(Canada St. 518-668-5471. Mid-May–mid-Oct.; adm. fee)*, where James Fenimore Cooper set *The Last of the Mohicans,* now surrounded by such attractions as Magic Forest and Splash World.

Return to Saratoga Springs via US 9, with a stop in Glens Fall to see the Hyde Collection (see sidebar p. 68).

Steamer on Lake George

Thousand Islands

● **150 miles** ● **3 to 4 days** ● **Spring through autumn**

Bordered by the U.S. and Canada, the Thousand Islands encompass a 50-mile stretch of the St. Lawrence Seaway northeast of Lake Ontario. Forested islands—some with castles—pepper ribbons of blue water. Ports and fortresses dot the mainlands, each with a story about the War of 1812 or rum-running.

Many travelers arrive at the Thousand Islands towing their boat, but even if you don't own one, this route puts you on the water. You'll begin on the shore at historic Sackets Harbor and head north along Lake Ontario to Cape Vincent, where ferries transport you and your car to Wolfe Island and on into Canada. Here, Kingston's active waterfront and Fort Henry will deepen your sense of maritime lifestyles, while in Gananoque you can shop for British imports or take a cruise to see why there's no official island count (one source claims there are 1,865 islands). The Thousand Islands Parkway northeast of Gananoque, along the river, will show you the islands from a landlubber's perspective, while the Thousand Islands International Bridge will provide a bird's-eye view. Back in the U.S., the tour continues to Alexandria Bay, which offers all the lures of a resort town as well as boat tours to sumptuous Boldt Castle. Complete the tour with two engaging museums in the northeastern part of the Thousand Islands region.

A clutch of federal-style buildings dominate ❶ **Sackets Harbor**★ ★ *(Chamber of Commerce 315-646-1700)*, where Americans twice repelled the British during the War of 1812. Learn the details at the **Sackets Harbor Battlefield** *(W. Main St. 315-646-3634. Museum open mid-May–Oct. Wed.-Sun., battlefield year-round)*, overlooking Lake Ontario. The Commandant's House has been restored to its 1860 condition, and living history docents encamped on the shore re-create the year 1812 and keep a wary eye out for British troops from Canada.

Nearby stands the **Sacket Mansion** *(301 W. Main St. 315-646-2321. Daily July-Aug., Wed.-Sat. Mem. Day–June and Sept.–Columbus Day)*, the Visitor Center for the New York State Heritage Area. Pick up a guide to the town's historic houses and set out on a walking tour. Along the way, you will notice that what looks—at first—to be a town lost in the past is actually full of lively possibilities. You can spend hours or even days in the antique stores and boutiques. The harbor with its sailing yachts is almost always in view.

Circling north on N.Y. 180 and west on N.Y. 12E, you

71

Among the Thousand Islands

Haying season along N.Y.12E, near Cape Vincent

will find a good place to watch the seaway ship traffic at **Tibbetts Point Lighthouse** *(Cty. Rd. 6, 3 miles W of Cape Vincent)*, marking the shore of the fishing village of ❷ **Cape Vincent** *(Chamber of Commerce 315-654-2481)*. During the summer, anglers flock to Cape Vincent's lakeshore in hopes of catching black bass, walleye, and pike. You can see some live specimens at the **Cape Vincent Fisheries Station-Aquarium** *(541 E. Broadway. 315-654-2147. Daily Mem. Day–Columbus Day, Mon.-Fri. May–Mem. Day and Columbus Day–Oct.)*. To immerse yourself in artifacts of years past, visit the **Cape Vincent Historical Museum** *(James St. 315-654-4400. July-Aug.; donation)*.

Then drive aboard **Horne's Ferry**★ *(Foot of James St. 315-783-0638. May-Oct.; fare)* for a St. Lawrence cruise to Canada and **Wolfe Island,** largest of the Thousand Islands. Take time to explore, since Wolfe Island is probably the only island community you'll visit unless you have brought your own boat.

Named for the general who defeated the French, Wolfe Island has settled into a state of suspended animation. Except for the village of **Marysville,** the island remains largely farmland just as it was 200 years ago. **Fargo's General Store** *(Main and Centre Sts.)* and **Wolfe Island Bakery** *(Main St.)* serve as social centers for Marysville's residents, who seem to be independent and creative folk: A holistic medicine clinic, three art studios, and the **Wolfe Island Summer Music Festival** *(613-385-2323. June-Sept.)* thrive here. Although there is only one restaurant—the **General Wolfe Hotel** *(Main St. 613-385-2611)*—island guests support a half-dozen inns, a campground, and five fishing services. "Police department" is not even in the vocabulary of the 1,200 islanders. Herein lies the charm of Thousand Island life: You can ignore the cyberspace age—but the bright lights of Kingston are just a short boat ride away.

Now hop the free government ferry *(Centre St., Marysville. 613-548-7227)* to Kingston. Once the capital of Canada, ❸ **Kingston**★★ is rich with maritime culture; the city calls itself the "freshwater sailing capital of the world," and you can see why if you walk down to the lake from the **Greater Kingston Tourist Information Center** *(209 Ontario St. 613-548-4415)*. Marinas, excursion boats, ferries, and Coast Guard vessels wrap around Kingston's waterfront.

While boats are a big attraction here, they are not the only game in town. As home to the Royal Military College and Queens University, a National Historic Site established in 1841, Kingston has the cosmopolitan flair of a college town. Summer visitors gravitate to the **Kingston Summer Festival** *(613-530-2050 or 800-615-5666. July–mid-Sept.; fee)*, featuring repertory theater, music ensembles, and comedy at the Grand Theatre *(218 Princess St.)*, as well as Shakespeare at Fort Henry. Outdoor cafés pepper Ontario Street and ethnic restaurants abound throughout town, which is also host to more than 20 museums.

Don't miss the **Marine Museum of the Great Lakes at Kingston**★ *(55 Ontario St. 613-542-2261. Adm. fee)*, which displays artifacts from sunken ships. You can tour the

Gananoque waterfront

Alexander Henry, an icebreaker that also operates as a B&B. The living history museum at **Fort Henry**★ *(Hwys. 2 and 15. 613-542-7388. Mid-May–Sept.; adm. fee)* re-creates garrison life in 1867 and gives an exceptional view of Kingston, the lake, and the Thousand Islands from its perch above Navy Bay. **Bellevue House National Historic Site** *(35 Centre St. 613-545-8666. April-Oct., by appt. rest of year; adm. fee)* is an Italianate villa that revives the mid-19th century, when Canada's first prime minister, Sir John A. Macdonald, lived here. Hockey fans will head for the **International Ice Hockey Federation Museum** *(York and*

Alfred Sts. 613-544-2355. June–Labor Day daily, by appt. rest of year; adm. fee). An easy way to see many of the historic sites is to take the **Confederation Trolley Tour** *(209 Ontario St. 613-548-4453. Mid-May–Labor Day daily, Sept. weekends; fare).*

About 25 miles east lies the heart of the Thousand Islands, ❹ **Gananoque**★ *(Chamber of Commerce 613-382-3250 or 800-561-1595).* Founded by Loyalists to the British Crown who crossed the river during the American Revolution, Gananoque (ganna-KNOCK-way) is perhaps best known as a jumping-off place for Thousand Island boat excursions *(Gananoque Boat Line, 6 Water St. 613-382-2144. May–mid-Oct.; fare).* The town itself has its own charms. You can explore the shops of **Historic 1000 Islands Village** *(Water St.),* a re-created 19th-century waterfront neighborhood, and look at island memorabilia and local artwork at the new **Arthur Child Heritage Center of the Thousand Islands** *(613-382-2535. Mid-May–Oct.; adm. fee),* part of the same complex.

If you want to stretch your legs, visit Confederation Park along the banks of the river that inspired the Indian name *Gananoque*—"place where water runs over rocks."

The trip's most scenic drive lies ahead. From Gananoque, follow the **Thousand Islands Parkway**★★ 25 miles (40 km) east for uninterrupted vistas of the St. Lawrence and the islands. A paved bicycle path runs

Speedboat cockpit, Antique Boat Museum, Clayton

along the road; if you don't have your own, the 1,000 Islands Camping Resort *(382 Thousand Islands Parkway, E of Gananoque. 613-659-3058. Mid-May–mid-Oct.)* rents bikes. Along the way, you will pass the village of **Rockport,** known for its artists' studios.

If you fancy a swim, stop by Mallorytown Landing, the mainland headquarters and campground for the ❺ **St. Lawrence Islands National Park**★ *(Cty. Rd. 5 and Hwy. 2. 613-923-5261. Adm. fee).* Comprised of 21 wilderness sites, the park is a collection of large and small islands sprinkling the river...where you can vanish for days or weeks if you have a boat.

Another way to see island wilderness is to backtrack to the foot of the **Thousand Islands International Bridge** *(Toll)* and take the elevator 400 feet to the top of the **Thousand Islands Skydeck** *(613-659-2335. Mid-April–Oct.;*

Boldt Castle, Heart Island

adm. fee) observation tower. For more views, stop off at
Wellesley Island State Park *(315-482-5842. Parking fee
June-Aug.),* accessible off the Thousand Islands International Bridge. The park's **Minna Anthony Common
Nature Center**★ encompasses a 600-acre wildlife sanctuary for hiking, as well as naturalist-led canoe excursions.
Six trails explore steep cliffs, wetlands, meadows, and
deep woods, offering sublime river overlooks. At the
nature center you'll find displays on the St. Lawrence
River environment, geology, flora, and fauna, plus collections of live native fish, reptiles, and amphibians. The
busy park also contains 429 campsites, eleven winterized
cabins, a nine-hole golf course, a marina, and a natural
sand beach.

Returning to the U.S. mainland, dip southwest 7 miles
on N.Y. 12 to ❻ **Clayton**★ *(Chamber of Commerce 315-
686-3771).* Shade trees, Victorian architecture, and outdoor concerts every summer Wednesday put you at ease.
Attractive shops, theatrical productions at the opera
house, and great fishing offer something for everyone. It
is claimed that Thousand Island dressing was first served
to the public here at the **Thousand Islands Inn** *(335
Riverside Dr. 315-686-3030).* And no water lover should
miss the outstanding collection of antique boats and
engines at the **Antique Boat Museum**★ *(750 Mary St.*

Remington's *The Broncho Buster,*
Frederic Remington Art Museum

Ship in a Box

Each year hundreds of thousands of tourists flock to the **Dwight D. Eisenhower Visitors' Center** and the **U.S. Eisenhower Lock** *(NE of Ogdensburg on N.Y. 37, then NE of Massena. 315-764-3200).* Ships from all over the world enter the Eisenhower Lock, and are raised or lowered 100 feet in 10 minutes to bypass the St. Lawrence River rapids. Two thousand lock transits occur here annually as ships carry cargo between lake ports and distant shores. You can learn the name, type, and estimated arrival time of ships on the Visitors' Center television monitor.

315-686-4104. Mid-May–mid-Oct.; adm. fee) or the decoy and muskie exhibits at the **Thousand Islands Museum of Clayton** *(403 Riverside Dr. 315-686-5794. Mem. Day–Labor Day; adm. fee).*

Northeast on N.Y. 12 lies the Thousand Islands' major resort town, ❼ **Alexandria Bay** *(Chamber of Commerce 315-482-9531).* Alex Bay pulses to the beat of open-air restaurants and boat engines. This is the land of bungee jumpers and go-cart racers, where lodgings for every taste and pocketbook abound. The best-known house around is **Boldt Castle** ★★ *(Heart Island. 315-482-2501 or 800-847-5263. Mid-May–mid-Oct.; adm. fee).* If you don't have a boat to take you out to Heart Island, catch a water taxi or a ride from Uncle Sam Boat Tours *(James St. 315-482-2611. May-Oct.; fare).*

A 120-room Rhineland fortress, Boldt Castle stands as a monument to love and heartbreak. Austrian immigrant George C. Boldt, a self-made millionaire and proprietor of the Waldorf-Astoria Hotel in New York City, conceived his monument in 1900 as a present to his wife, Louise. In 1904 Louise Boldt died of a heart attack before work was finished on the castle, and Boldt never returned to Heart Island, having spent two million dollars on his dream. In a state of disrepair, the castle eventually fell into the hands of the International Bridge Authority, which has been restoring the castle and boathouse since 1977, filling the main floors with exhibits reviving the islands' Golden Age.

To get off the beaten path, follow N.Y. 12 farther northeast to **Morristown,** the home of a friendly café called **Joe's Grub** *(Main St. 315-375-8408),* kids wandering the streets with fishing poles, and one the funkiest museums you are ever likely to visit. The **Red Barn Museum** *(River Rd. E. 315-375-6390. Late June–Aug. weekends, and by appt.; donation)* is the town historian's collection of costumes and artifacts depicting life in the Thousand Islands. Each display sits in a stall in the rambling barn, and you are likely to get an anecdotal tour from the historian.

Wrap up your drive with another worthy museum just northeast in the river town of ❽ **Ogdensburg.** The **Frederic Remington Art Museum** *(303 Washington St. 315-393-2425. May-Oct. daily, Nov.-April Tues.-Sun.; adm. fee)* showcases oils, watercolors, sketches, and bronzes by the artist who glorified the American frontier. Afterward, stroll along the shore and watch the ships disappear among the islands.

Finger Lakes★

● 160 miles ● 2 to 3 days ● Spring through autumn

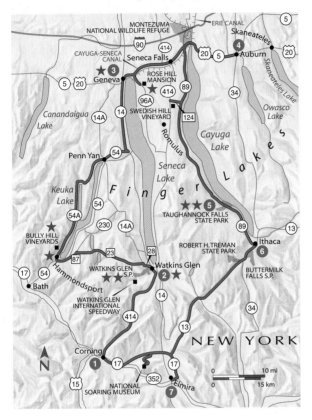

The slivers of water that fan out to form the Finger Lakes were carved long ago by glaciers or...as the Iroquois who inhabited the area believed, by the hand of the Great Spirit. Stretching from the shores of Lake Ontario to the Pennsylvania border, the region today offers a survey of natural and human creations to inspire the spirit and calm the mind. The drive begins with the many offerings of the Corning Glass Center. Then it loops around the three central Finger Lakes—Keuka, Seneca, and Cayuga—through rolling hills quilted with farms and more than 45 vineyards. This is the East Coast's equivalent to California's Napa Valley—as the number of wineries continues to grow, so does the sophistication of the wine.

While the whole trip could become a tasting tour, historic resort villages such as Hammondsport and Geneva offer lakeside recreation and other diversions. There are natural wonders along this route as well—the lakes

Glassware, Corning Glass Center

themselves, but also dramatic chasms such as Watkins Glen and 215-foot Taughannock Falls. The drive explores Ithaca, home of Cornell University and a small city in its own right, set among the hills, gorges, and woods that were once at the very heart of the Iroquois Confederation. The last stop is Elmira, where Mark Twain wrote *Huckleberry Finn,* among other works.

Your first stop in the town of ❶ **Corning** should be its **Visitor Center** *(Historic District exit off N.Y. 17. 607-936-4686),* where you can pick up maps and brochures, including some on the Finger Lakes region. The big attraction, the **Corning Glass Center**★ *(Centerway and Museum Way. 607-974-8271. Adm. fee),* is just up the street in a glass-and-steel complex. You can see ancient and modern glasswork at the Corning Museum; hands-on displays in the Hall of Science and Industry; and crafts people in the Steuben Factory who transform gobs of molten glass into art. If you want to avoid the crowds, arrive early and spend midday exploring the shops, galleries, and restaurants of **Historic Market Street.** Also in Corning is the **Rockwell Museum** *(City Hall, 11 Cedar St. 607-937-5386. June-Sept.; adm. fee),* with its collections of Western art, Indian artifacts, and Steuben glass.

North of Corning on N.Y. 414, the town of ❷ **Watkins**

Glen★ is an apt place for a first encounter with a Finger Lake—beautiful Seneca Lake. By day, sail and power vessels carry passengers from the marina out for a quiet day on the 35-mile-long lake. For wilder water, visit **Watkins Glen State Park**★★ *(Franklin St. 607-535-4511. Park year-round, gorge June–early Nov.; adm. fee Mem. Day–Oct.)*, where the 1.5-mile Gorge Trail travels over bridges and under falls while climbing through the narrow and deep chasm to the top of 300-foot cliffs. A popular nighttime attraction, the **Timespell Sound, Light, and Laser Show** *(607-535-4960 or 800-853-7735. Mid-May–mid-Oct.; adm. fee)* takes place in the spectacular gorge and showcases its geological formation.

The town is also famous for sports car and stock car racing at **Watkins Glen International Speedway** *(2790 Cty. Rd. 16. 607-535-2481. June-Sept., call for race schedule; adm. fee)*. Racing fans camp on the speedway's infield, but campers in search of a modicum of peace will opt for the KOA facility *(N.Y. 414, 4.5 miles S of Watkins Glen. 607-535-7404. Mid-April–mid-Oct.; fee)*. The campground, like the rest of the town, can be overwhelmed on race weekends *(June-Sept.)*, when as many as 200,000 fans descend on the town.

Motorists heading west from Watkins Glen to **Hammondsport**★ enjoy one of the many undulating drives through emerald countryside characteristic of the Finger Lakes region. As N.Y. 54 descends into the village poised at the edge of Keuka Lake, travelers at early autumn harvest time will get their first tangy scent of grapes.

The quaint town of Hammondsport is the commercial center for the area's wine industry. Stop at the **Chamber of Commerce** *(56 Main St. 607-569-2989. Mon.-Fri.)* to get a complete list of area vineyards. Then check out the **Wine and Grape Museum of Greyton H. Taylor** *(8843 G.H.T. Memorial Dr., off N.Y. 54A. 607-868-4814. May-Oct.; adm. fee)* to learn more

Appeal to the Great Spirit, Rockwell Art Museum in Corning

about the industry before taking off to tour your choice of 11 different vineyards. The one adjacent to the museum, **Bully Hill Vineyards**★ *(607-868-3610. Tours*

Keuka Lake landscape

mid-May–Oct.), was begun by Walter S. Taylor in the late 1960s in reaction to the corporate takeovers of area vineyards. Today Bully Hill is known for its hybrid wines and unusual labels.

Anyone interested in vintage aircraft or motorcycles should stop at the **Glenn H. Curtiss Museum of Local History** *(8419 N.Y. 54. 607-569-2160. Adm. fee).* On view is a collection of inventions by Curtiss—the "Father of Naval Aviation"—including a "Jenny" biplane. Dinner cruises aboard the ***Keuka Maid*** *(N.Y. 54, Hammondsport. 607-569-3631. May-Oct.; fare. Reservations recommended)* make for a romantic evening with cottage lights winking through the darkness.

The look is elegant as you approach ❸ **Geneva**★ *(Chamber of Commerce 315-789-1776),* at Seneca Lake's northern end. Spend the night or just stop for a meal at the Romanesque **Belhurst Castle** *(N.Y. 14. 315-781-0201)* or the nearby Renaissance villa, **Geneva on the Lake** *(1001 Lochland Rd. 315-789-1555).* Other estates line the lakeshore as you skirt the campuses of Hobart and William Smith Colleges and descend into the town's historic district. Here stands the **Smith Opera House** *(82 Seneca St. 315-781-5483)* along with Gothic cottages, Greek Revival houses, and federal-style row houses, including the **Prouty-Chew House** *(543 S. Main St. 315-789-5151. Closed Sun.-Mon.*

Sept.-June). Built in 1829, it contains period rooms and the Geneva Historical Society's museum.

Just east of town grandly rises **Rose Hill Mansion** ★ *(N.Y. 96A. 315-789-3848. May-Oct.; adm. fee).* Ionic columns front this 21-room historic landmark, considered one of America's finest Greek Revival houses. Built by Gen. William K. Strong in 1839, the mansion has been restored to its original era.

Rose Hill Mansion, near Geneva

East of Geneva, US 20/N.Y. 5 follows the **Cayuga-Seneca Canal,** a branch of the Erie Canal linking the two largest Finger Lakes. In warm weather the canal and its locks bustle with private watercraft as well as rented canal boats *(Mid-Lakes Navigation, Cold Springs Harbor Marina, Cold Springs. 315-685-8500 or 800-545-4318. Mid-May–mid-Oct.)* that cruise the wine country.

Nearby **Seneca Falls** *(Chamber of Commerce 315-568-2906)* is a popular port of call. Here, Elizabeth Cady Stanton, Lucretia Mott, and others staked their claim for an equal share of the good life during the Seneca Falls Convention of 1848. The **Women's Rights National Historical Park** *(136 Fall St. 315-568-2991. Adm. fee)* marks the gathering site with interactive exhibits and a film on the history of the women's movement. Nearby, the **National Women's Hall of Fame** *(76 Fall St. 315-568-8030. Closed Mon.-Tues. Oct.-April; adm. fee)* honors more than 130 American women with photos and biographical sketches. The Seneca Falls Historical Society's museum *(55 Cayuga St. 315-568-8412. June-Sept. daily, Oct.-May Mon.-Fri.)* explores the town's past in period rooms, archives, and exhibits.

Harriet Tubman statue, at Women's Rights National Historical Park, Seneca Falls

Beyond Seneca Falls, a natural oasis along US 20 and the canal is the **Montezuma National Wildlife Refuge** *(315-568-5987),* over 7,000 acres of resting and nesting area in the middle of one the Atlantic flyway's busiest paths. In addition to a large variety of migratory waterfowl, the refuge hosts resident bald eagles as well.

Nine miles east in ❹ **Auburn** is the **Harriet Tubman Home** *(180 South St. 315-252-2081. Tues.-Fri.; donation),*

Skinny Atlas Sights

If you like mimosa brunches aboard a lake "steamer," polo matches, sailboat races, boutique shopping, champagne sunsets from a hot air balloon, and chamber music under the stars, make a date with "Skinny Atlas." Spelled Skaneateles, this village about a half-hour drive east of Seneca Falls looks and feels more like a Swiss spa than a New York lake port. Here you find a host of elegant B&Bs, shops, and restaurants. If you do nothing else here, consider boarding the *Barbara S. Wiles* (Mid-Lakes Navigation, Clift Park, Genesee St. 315-685-6600 or 800-545-4318) for her mail route around the lake. Or catch some sun and people-watch over lunch on the lakeside deck of the **Bluewater Grill** (11 W. Genesee St. 315-685-6600). If you're here in August, try for tickets to one of the Saturday concerts of the **Skaneateles Festival** (Brook Farm, 2870 W. Lake Rd. 315-685-7418), held outdoors.

82

where the famous escaped slave lived after the Civil War. The white clapboard house contains some of her possessions, and a tape describes her courageous role in leading more than 300 slaves to freedom. Tubman purchased the house with help from William H. Seward, Lincoln's secretary of state. His former residence, the 1816 **Seward House** (33 South St. 315-252-1283. April-Dec. Tues.-Sat.; adm. fee), holds original furnishings and documents, including some referring to "Seward's Folly," the purchase of Alaska in 1867.

On N.Y. 89, the route south along Cayuga's western shore to Ithaca claims seven wineries offering tours and tastings. Each vineyard has an unusual success story, and you may hear a rags-to-riches tale from the vintner at **Swedish Hill Vineyard** (Off N.Y. 124 on N.Y. 414, Romulus. 315-549-8326. Tours May-Oct., tastings year-round).

When the glacier-carved Cayuga Lake receded 10,000 years ago, the rim of hills and cliffs set the stage to make the Ithaca area a place of waterfalls and gorges. Just before reaching town, stop at ❺ **Taughannock Falls State Park**★★ (N.Y. 89. 607-387-6739. Parking fee in summer), a superb place to picnic. A road and trails lead to the top of the 215-foot falls, higher than those at Niagara. Smaller **Ithaca Falls** (Lake St., off N.Y. 34) rumbles through a gorge at the town's northeast corner. On Ithaca's southern edge, the cascades at **Buttermilk Falls State Park** (N.Y. 13. 607-273-5761. Parking fee late spring–early fall) attract picnickers, hikers, and campers, as does nearby **Robert H. Treman State Park** (N.Y. 13. 607-273-3440. Parking fee late spring–early fall).

A city of over 50,000 people when you include its 20,000 college students, ❻ **Ithaca** is an easy place to get lost.

Sailing on Lake Skaneateles

Stop at the **Visitor Center** *(904 E. Shore Dr., off N.Y. 13. 607-272-1313 or 800-284-8422. Mid-May–Oct. Mon.-Sat., Nov.–mid-May Mon.-Fri.)* to get local maps or book a room at one of the historic B&Bs. The towers of Ithaca's main attraction, **Cornell University★** *(University Ave. 607-254-4636)*, rise from the woods on the town's northeastern hills. Considered one of America's prettiest campuses, Cornell covers 745 acres.

You can walk in the footsteps of such famous Cornell faculty as I.M. Pei and Carl Sagan; stroll through the 3,000 acres of gardens and woodlands in the **Cornell Plantations** *(1 Plantations Rd. 607-255-3020)*; or go birding at the university's ornithological "lab," **Sapsucker Woods Sanctuary** *(N.Y. 13, N of town. 607-256-5056. Donation)*. At the heart of

Clock tower, Cornell University

campus, people linger near the **clock tower** to hear the carillon concerts or visit the **Herbert F. Johnson Museum of Art** ★ *(Central and University Aves. 607-255-6464. Mon.-Fri.)*. Called "the sewing machine" because of its radical design by I.M. Pei, the museum offers excellent views as well as one of the country's best university art collections.

N.Y. 13 and N.Y. 17 lead southwest through farm country to the last stop on this loop, **❼ Elmira** *(Chamber of Commerce 607-374-5137)*, where Mark Twain found peace and inspiration. Visit the **Mark Twain Study** ★ *(N. Main St. 607-735-1941. July-Aug.)*, on the Elmira College campus, where the author retreated to write *Huckleberry Finn*. Students give anecdotal history on Twain and his wife, native Elmiran Olivia Langdon. The author's grave rests at **Woodlawn Cemetery** *(1200 Walnut St. 607-732-0151)*, adjacent to

Sailplane somewhere above Elmira

Woodlawn National Cemetery *(607-732-5411)*, where thousands of Confederate prisoners are buried.

Also in town, the **Arnot Art Museum** *(235 Lake St. 607-734-3697. Closed Mon.; adm. fee)* features a strong collection of Dutch, Flemish, and French paintings. Elmira is a popular gliding center, and the exhibits and collection of sailplanes at the **National Soaring Museum** *(Off N.Y. 17, at 51 Soaring Hill Rd. 607-734-3128. July-Aug. Tues.-Sun.; adm. fee)* will leave you feeling free as a bird.

Return to Corning on N.Y. 17 west.

Niagara Country ★

● **230 miles** ● **3 to 4 days** ● **Spring through autumn**

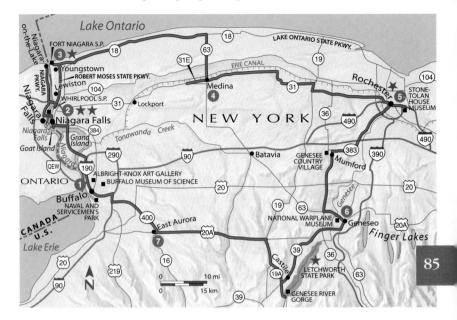

Water's the theme here. It binds Niagara Country together, providing a path for adventure between the second and third largest cities in New York—Buffalo and Rochester. At the start of this loop, you see how Buffalo owes its existence to the confluence of Lake Erie, the Niagara River, and the Erie Canal. Next the drive heads north along the Niagara River, joining the millions drawn to the falls. Where the Niagara meets Lake Ontario, the route visits Fort Niagara, witness to the important role the waterways played during the War of 1812. Along the Erie Canal a mule-drawn boat carries you back to the 1830s. Later, see Rochester's High Falls on the Genesee River, a focal point for a historic district. Following the river south, visit Letchworth State Park and the Genesee River Gorge—the "Grand Canyon of the East." The tour ends at the home of President Millard Fillmore, who presided over Oliver Hazard Perry's seafaring expedition to Japan.

A struggling frontier village, ❶ **Buffalo** boomed after the Erie Canal opened in 1825, and Great Lakes steamboats began hauling freight and settlers west. To appreciate the city's maritime setting, drive along I-190, poised between the shoreline and the cityscape. The vistas here inspired French settlers' name for their outpost: "Buffalo" is probably a corruption of *beau fleuve,* or beautiful river.

Theodore Roosevelt Inaugural N.H.S.

Dying to Jump

A legend in his own mind, Sam Patch (1807-1829) made a short but celebrated career of tempting fate by being the first man known to have survived Niagara Falls. He dove not once, but twice from Goat Island to the base of the falls. Patch liked to boast "some things can be done as well as others," and in this spirit decided to dive over Rochester's High Falls from a 20-foot platform erected on an island near Brown's Race. On Friday, November 13, 1829, Patch took the dive. His body did not surface until the next spring.

From the Church Street exit, follow signs to the **Visitor Information Center** *(Market Arcade, 617 Main St. 716-852-2356 or 888-228-3369)*. Park at the lot off Washington Street, pick up a walking guide to this city loaded with architectural monuments, and ride the metro for free along the 8-block Main Street pedestrian mall. Don't miss the art deco **City Hall** ★ *(65 Niagara Sq. 716-851-4200. Mon.-Fri.)*, built between 1929 and 1931 and one of the country's most spectacular public buildings. The view from the 28th floor gives you a sense of greater Buffalo, home to more than a million people. Right in front of City Hall stands the **McKinley Monument,** a 93-foot obelisk designed by Carrère and Hastings and named after the President, who was assassinated while visiting here in 1901.

You may want to linger in the **Theatre District** ★ *(Main St. bet. Tupper and Chippewa Sts. 716-852-2356 for event schedules and locations)* to dine and see a show. This collection of refurbished Gilded Age theaters, including the classic **Shea's Performing Arts Center** *(646 Main St. 716-847-1410)*, is a hub for sidewalk cafés as well as the theater scene. If it's antiques you want, more than 20 shops await, scattered between Virginia and North Streets in the funky **Historic Allentown** neighborhood.

Then head for the strong 19th- and 20th-century collection at the **Albright-Knox Art Gallery** *(1285 Elmwood Ave. 716-882-8700. Closed Mon.; adm. fee)*, featuring works by Picasso, van Gogh, Matisse, Renoir, and others. Dinosaurs are the primary draw at the **Buffalo Museum of Science** *(1020 Humboldt Pkwy. 716-896-5200. Closed Mon.; adm. fee)*, while the **Buffalo and Erie County Historical Society** *(25 Nottingham Ct. 716-872-9644. Closed Mon.; adm. fee)* offers a re-creation of an 1870s street and a symbolic edifice from the 1901 Pan-American Exposition.

Learn about President William McKinley's assassination and Theodore Roosevelt's dramatic swearing in at the Wilcox Mansion, now the **Theodore Roosevelt Inaugural National Historic Site** *(641 Delaware Ave. 716-884-0095. Closed Sat. Jan.-March; adm. fee)*. This estate is part of **Millionaires' Row,** where Buffalo's aristocrats lived and hosted the nation's leaders. You will find just as much wealth, but a very different style, at

the **Darwin D. Martin House** *(125 Jewett Pkwy. 716-829-2406. Under restoration),* designed by Frank Lloyd Wright in 1904; it's one of his several Buffalo masterpieces.

Enjoy a picnic or a waterfront stroll along **Erie Boulevard,** where paths and parkland skirt the yachts and condos at the Erie Basin Marina. Nearby, the **Naval and Servicemen's Park** *(1 Naval Park Cove, at foot of Pearl and Main Sts. 716-847-1773. Daily April-Oct., weekends in Nov.; adm. fee)* has a collection of warplanes and ships to explore, including the USS *Little Rock,* a missile cruiser; USS *The Sullivans,* a destroyer; and the USS *Croaker,* a submarine.

Then follow I-190 north to the city of ❷ **Niagara Falls**★★ *(Information Center 716-284-2000 or 800-421-5223).* Just about everything you have ever heard about the carnival atmosphere here is probably true. Hosting over 12 million visitors a year, this is a world-class attraction, with development to match: Viewing towers rise above the falls like giant mushrooms; hotels crowd the river roads; T-shirt shops and nightclubs abound; wax museums, fast food franchises, and factory outlet malls fight for space.

87

Still—the falls can make you forget everything except the sights and sounds of 700,000 gallons of water crashing over 184-foot cliffs each second. There are actually three cataracts: American and Bridal Veil Falls on the American side, and Horseshoe Falls on the Canadian side. The closest

Observation deck at Niagara Falls

views of the American Falls are found in **Niagara Reservation State Park** *(716-285-3891. Parking fee in summer)*, located south of town via the Robert Moses State Parkway. Walk or drive over the bridge to **Goat Island,** which divides American Falls and Bridal Veil Falls from Horseshoe Falls. There are two big parking lots, a good bit of green space for picnics, and trails leading along the river's edge to places such as **Luna Island** *(Accessible by footbridge bet. American and Bridal Veil Falls)*, at the brink of the crashing waters.

If you want to feel the power of the falls, go down to their base. The easiest way is to take the guided **Cave of the Winds Trip**★★ *(Goat Island. 716-278-1730. June-Oct.; adm. fee)*, which starts with an elevator ride from Goat Island down through the escarpment to the base of Bridal Veil Falls. Here you follow a wooden walkway to within 25 feet of the cascade. The 282-foot **Prospect Point Observation Tower**★ *(Prospect Park. 716-278-1703. April-Jan., weather permitting; adm. fee)* rises a hundred feet above the cliffs to offer above and below vistas of the American Falls and upper rapids from the U.S. shore.

You can also go across to the Canadian side and see the Horseshoe Falls and the Niagara River at **Table Rock House**★ *(Niagara Pkwy., 1 mile S of Rainbow Bridge. 905-358-3268. Adm. fee)*, where three tunnels take you to spectacular vistas. But the most thrilling way to view the falls is aboard the ***Maid of the Mist***★★ boats *(American dock at Prospect Pt., Canadian dock at Clifton St. and River Rd. 716-284-8897 or 905-358-5781. Mid-May–mid-Oct.; fare)*, which chug to the base of the cascades and pass directly in front of the three falls.

If you are short on time, can't walk far, or hate waiting in long lines, consider taking a tour. The simplest way is via the sightseeing trains of Niagara Viewmobiles *(Goat Island and Prospect Pt. 716-278-1730. June–mid-Nov.; fare)*, which drop you

Fort Niagara State Park

off at sights on the American side. Bedore Tours *(Howard Johnson's, Main St. 716-285-5261. May–early Nov.; fare)* earns high marks for its variety of van tours to popular attractions.

To truly escape the crowds and hype, head north on

the Robert Moses State Parkway to the **Schoellkopf Geological Museum** *(Moses Pkwy., 1 mile N of Rainbow Bridge. 716-278-1780. Closed Mon.-Wed. Nov.-March; adm. fee),* also part of the state park. An audiovisual show explains how the falls have evolved over the last 12,000 years. Nearby **Whirlpool State Park** *(Moses Pkwy. 716-285-7740)* offers nature trails and views overlooking the whirlpool created by the Niagara River's 90-degree turn and the gorge.

George Eastman House, Rochester

Now take a jaunt into Ontario across the Whirlpool Rapids Bridge, and go north on the Niagara Parkway to the **Great Gorge Adventure**★ *(4330 Niagara Pkwy. 905-374-1221. Late April–mid-Oct.; adm. fee).* Here you can ride an elevator to the lower Niagara River and see some of the world's fiercest rapids. Theater lovers flock to **Niagara-on-the-Lake** *(Chamber of Commerce 905-468-4263),* a polished Tudor-style beach resort where the river meets Lake Ontario. The resort plays host to the **Shaw Festival** *(10 Queen's Parade, off Niagara Pkwy. 905-468-2172 or 800-511-SHAW. April-Oct.; adm. fee),* the second largest repertory theater company in North America. It produces plays by George Bernard Shaw and his contemporaries in three theaters.

Return to the U.S. side across the Lewiston-Queenston Bridge, and jog south on the Robert Moses State Parkway to the **Niagara Power Project Visitors Center** *(N.Y. 104. 716-285-3211 ext. 6660).* The center provides a great view of the gorge as well as a film and models that illustrate hydroelectric power on the Niagara, site of the world's first hydro station. Currently 50 to 70 percent of the river's volume is siphoned off for power generation before spilling over the falls.

Then backtrack north to tranquil **Lewiston,** perched on the escarpment above the Niagara. Here, explore **Earl W. Brydges Artpark** *(150 S. Fourth St. 716-754-4375 or 800-659-PARK. May-Sept.).* The 200-acre state park along the Niagara River features working artists, modern sculpture gardens, wandering musicians, and outdoor stage productions.

Just a few miles north on Lake Ontario stands ❸ **Fort Niagara State Park**★ *(N.Y. 18F, Youngstown. 716-745-7273. Summer parking fee).* The 504 acres here encompass Old

Fort Niagara and an 18th-century French-style castle. Drills and ceremonies occur daily from July through Labor Day, and reenactments by period militia illustrate the conflict that boiled up and down the Niagara River during the French and Indian War, the American Revolution, and the War of 1812. The surrounding park is a popular place for boating, fishing, swimming, and picnicking.

Less than an hour's drive east brings you into Erie Canal country at **4 Medina.** You can view the canal and learn its history aboard the ***Miss Apple Grove*** *(Apple Grove Inn, N.Y. 31E, W of Medina. 716-798-2323. May-Oct.; fare).* The two-hour cruises on the mule-drawn barge include banjo sing-alongs, historical narrations, and entertaining mule skinners.

Move on to **5 Rochester**★ and get oriented at the **Visitor Information Center** *(126 Andrews St. 716-546-3070)* in the restored **Brown's Race Historic District**★ *(Bounded by Central Ave., Factory and State Sts., and Genesee River),* which also offers a market, historic iron forge, and the 96-foot High Falls on the Genesee River. On summer nights, watch the **River of Light** *(Mid-May–Sept.)* laser and fireworks show at the High Falls from the **Granite Mills Commons** park *(bet. Pont de Rennes pedestrian bridge and Center at High Falls).* The **Center at High Falls** *(60 Brown's Race. 716-325-2030. Wed.-Sun.),* an educational entertainment center with 3-D exhibits, shows how geology, technology, culture, and creativity have influenced life in this city.

At the Genesee Country Village

Three of the city's most popular attractions are located on East Avenue. Exhibits at the **Rochester Museum & Science Center** *(657 East Ave. 716-271-1880. Adm. fee)* interpret colonial and Native American relations. The **George Eastman House**★★ *(900 East Ave. 716-271-3361. Closed Mon. June-April; adm. fee)* has recently been restored to show the 50-room colonial revival mansion and gardens as they were when the founder of Kodak lived here, in the early 20th century. In the attached **International Museum of Photography and Film** you can see works of virtually all the great photographers—including Matthew Brady's Civil War images—as well as view contemporary and classic films at the two theaters *(call for show times).* Down the street, the **Stone-Tolan House Museum** *(2370 East Ave. 716-546-7029. Fri.-Sun.; adm. fee)* offers guided tours to visitors curious about how the Stone family managed their 1805 tavern, farm, smokehouse, and orchard.

Two museums celebrate remarkable Rochester women. The **Susan B. Anthony House** *(17 Madison St.*

716-235-6124. Thurs.-Sat.; adm. fee) lets you tour where the libertarian launched her anti-slavery campaign, lobbied for women's rights, and was arrested for voting. **The Margaret Woodbury Strong Museum** *(1 Manhattan Sq. 716-263-2700. Adm. fee)* delights visitors with interactive displays illustrating cultural history since 1820 with more than 500,000 items depicting everyday American life and what may be the world's largest collection of dolls and dollhouses.

Drive some 20 miles southwest of Rochester via N.Y. 383 to **Mumford** and the **Genesee Country Village** *(Off N.Y. 36. 716-538-6822. May-Oct. Tues.-Sun.; adm. fee)*. This is a good place to gain insight into the history of the largely rural Genesee River Valley, as crafts people and costumed interpreters re-create the evolution of a 19th-century farm and village in a 57-building complex.

Another 20 miles south at ❻ **Geneseo,** aviation enthusiasts will find the **National Warplane Museum** *(Flint Hill Rd. at the Geneseo Airport. 716-243-2242. Adm. fee)* a must stop. Here (unless

Genesee River Gorge

they're at an air show) await a squadron of such World War II combat aircraft as the B-17 Flying Fortress and PBY-6A Catalina, in flying condition.

Next follow N.Y. 39 to N.Y. 19A, which leads to Castile and **Letchworth State Park** ★ *(716-493-3600. May-Oct.; adm. fee)*. Relax and enjoy these 14,350 acres of wilderness surrounding the 600-foot-deep **Genesee River Gorge.** It is complemented by three major waterfalls, fishing, hiking, white-water rafting, canoeing, swimming pools, campsites, cabins, and a country inn.

Driving west on US 20A, you'll reach the last stop on this loop, ❼ **East Aurora** and the **Millard Fillmore House** *(24 Shearer Ave. 716-652-8875. June–mid-Oct. Wed. and Sat.-Sun.; adm. fee)*. Fillmore built this five-room cottage when he was starting a family with his bride Abigail. The house, Fillmore's furniture, and a few documents speak of the humble beginnings and romantic dreams of this man, the undereducated son of a farmer who became his nation's 13th President.

Return to Buffalo via N.Y. 400 and I-190.

Lake Erie and the Alleghenies

● 300 miles ● 3 to 4 days ● Late spring through autumn

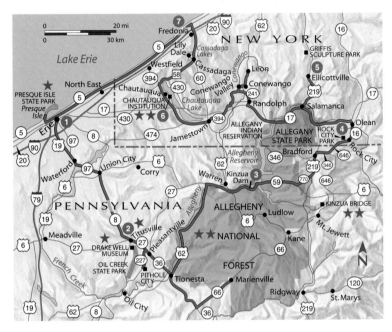

Looping through the deeply wooded mountains of northwestern Pennsylvania and southwestern New York, this drive showcases a remote landscape sprinkled with intriguing pockets of culture. Beginning in Erie, where the brig USS *Niagara* flies its battle flag over Lake Erie, the route slowly climbs toward the thick forest and fishing

Along the Presque Isle Peninsula, Erie

streams of Allegheny National Forest. Along the way you discover Titusville, where the modern petroleum industry began. Farther into the mountains await Kinzua Dam and the Allegheny Reservoir, projects that pitted the government against the Seneca Indians for decades.

You cross into New York, where the Alleghenies give way to a gentler landscape of lakes, hills, and farms. Here, almost every valley remains a refuge for proud communities, from the Seneca Indians at Salamanca to the Amish farmers of Conewango Valley to the religious idealists at Chautauqua Lake to Lily Dale's free thinkers. The drive ends along Lake Erie's shoreline, one of the East's largest and finest grape-growing regions.

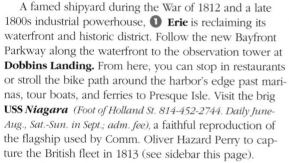

Napping on the Oil Creek & Titusville Railroad

A famed shipyard during the War of 1812 and a late 1800s industrial powerhouse, ❶ **Erie** is reclaiming its waterfront and historic district. Follow the new Bayfront Parkway along the waterfront to the observation tower at **Dobbins Landing.** From here, you can stop in restaurants or stroll the bike path around the harbor's edge past marinas, tour boats, and ferries to Presque Isle. Visit the brig **USS *Niagara*** *(Foot of Holland St. 814-452-2744. Daily June-Aug., Sat.-Sun. in Sept.; adm. fee),* a faithful reproduction of the flagship used by Comm. Oliver Hazard Perry to capture the British fleet in 1813 (see sidebar this page).

Heading up State Street to the center of town, stop at the new **Discovery Square** cultural complex, which encompasses the **Erie Art Museum** *(411 State St. 814-459-5477. Closed Mon.; adm. fee);* the **Erie History Center** *(417-421 State St. 814-454-1813. Tues.-Sat.; donation),* offering guided tours of the 1839 Cashiers House and a restored Greek Revival town house; the **Experience Children's Museum** *(420 French St. 814-453-3743. July-Aug. Tues.-Sun., Sept.-June Wed.-Sun.; adm. fee);* and performance facilities for music, theater, and dance.

While on State Street, pause at the **Visitors Bureau** *(1006 State St. 814-454-7191)* for information on the city's various historical sites, including the **Wayne Blockhouse** *(560 E. 3rd St. 814-871-4531),* a reproduction of the blockhouse where "Mad" Anthony Wayne, a Revolutionary War general, died in 1796.

Don't miss the **Erie Historical Museum & Planetarium** *(356 W. 6th St. 814-871-5790. Sept.-May Tues.-Sun.; adm. fee),* housed in an industrial magnate's 1891 mansion.

Don't Give Up the Ship

The Battle of Lake Erie stands out more for its rhetoric than its military aplomb. On September 10, 1813, Comm. Oliver Hazard Perry and his nine ships engaged a British fleet near Sandusky, Ohio. As the battle raged, Perry's flotilla suffered 123 casualties, and his flagship the *Lawrence* was disabled. But far from surrendering, Perry transferred to the brig *Niagara,* raised his "Don't Give Up the Ship!" battle flag, and fought on. Following the conflict, he wrote his famous dispatch to Gen. William Henry Harrison: "We have met the enemy and they are ours."

With its fancy woodwork, friezes, and stained-glass windows, the house alone is worth the visit. Self-guided tours showcase period settings and exhibits on regional and city history.

To free your spirit, head for **Presque Isle State Park**★

Autumn color in Allegany State Park

(Pa. 832, off Alt. Pa. 5. 814-833-7424). The drive around the 3,200-acre peninsula is nearly 14 miles, taking you along developed and undeveloped beaches, wetlands, hiking trails, and picnic sites. The interpretive center *(Pa. 832. 814-833-0351. Mem. Day–Labor Day, call for off-season schedule)* has ecological and nature exhibits.

As US 19 climbs south out of the coastal plain into the Allegheny foothills, you pass through a region rich in French and Indian War history. In **Waterford,** the **Fort LeBoeuf Museum** *(123 S. High St. 814-723-2573. Call for schedule)* has detailed models of the Iroquois village and French fort that stood here in the 1700s. In 1753 a young George Washington (then a major in the Virginia militia) delivered an ultimatum to the French demanding they withdraw from the area. The French refused, and the heightened tensions led to the French and Indian War.

From Waterford, go southeast on Pa. 97 and Pa. 8 to

the tiny lumber town of ❷ **Titusville**★**,** where the oil industry was revolutionized virtually overnight. Attempting to improve the flow of a commercial oil spring in 1859, Col. Edwin Drake and a creative blacksmith named William "Uncle Billy" Smith drilled a gusher—the world's first successful oil well. Thus began the modern petroleum age, and Pennsylvania became the country's top oil producer for nearly 30 years. The **Drake Well Museum**★ *(S of town at E. Bloss St. and Allen St. extension, off Pa. 8. 814-827-2797. May-Oct. daily, Nov.-April Tues.-Sun.; adm. fee)* has a reproduction of the engine house and derrick, along with a collection of other period drilling equipment and artifacts. A film and photo collection document the oil boom that overwhelmed the rural valley. At the museum you can board the **Oil Creek & Titusville Railroad** *(814-676-1733. Wed.-Sun. July-Aug. and Oct., Sat.-Sun. Sept.; fare),* which transports passengers to the heart of oil country with 2.5-hour round-trip train rides in restored 1930s passenger cars.

To learn about an oil boom town that flourished during the late 1860s, go east on Pa. 27 and south on Pa. 227 to **Pithole City.** No buildings remain, but the **Pithole Visitors Center** *(Pa. 227, S of Pleasantville. 814-827-2797. June–Labor Day Wed.-Sun.; adm. fee)* uses a video, model, and maps to introduce travelers to the vanished town. A self-guided walking tour brochure leads visitors past cellar holes, old streets, and abandoned wells.

Leaving oil country, the drive travels south on Pa. 36 to the western edge of the **Allegheny National Forest**★★ *(814-723-5150).* Extending 40 miles south from the New York–Pennsylvania border, the 513,000-acre forest contains fishing lakes and rushing rivers. In the village of **Tionesta,** the **Visitor Center** *(422 Elm St., near the US 62 bridge. 814-755-3338. Mem. Day–Labor Day)* has information on hiking, camping, and canoeing opportunities.

A great way to plumb the heart of the national forest is by steam train. Take Pa. 36 and Pa. 66 east to Marienville, where the **Knox & Kane Railroad**★ *(Pa. 66. 814-927-6621. Tues.-Sun. July-Aug., Fri.-Sat. June and Sept., Wed.-Sun. in Oct.; fare)* offers 32- and 96-mile trips through the mountains and over 2,053-foot **Kinzua Bridge**★★**,** the world's highest railroad viaduct when completed in 1882. Towering 300 feet above Kinzua Creek, it was dubbed by local citizens the "eighth wonder of the world." It's now a state park. The railroad also offers travelers the chance to camp overnight aboard a caboose.

Native American dancer at Ludlow

Amish country, Conewango Valley

Sculpture Grows Like Weeds

Just off US 219 north of Ellicottville, you will find a 400-acre nature preserve that is not only a sanctuary for flora and fauna, but also for 200 very large pieces of sculpture. **Griffis Sculpture Park** *(W of US 219 on Ahrens and Rohr Hill Rds. 716-257-9344. Donation)* offers 10 miles of hiking trails where walkers encounter everything from a monster mosquito and giant mushrooms to towering Picassolike human forms. Really strange!

Backtrack to US 62 and follow it north along the riffling Allegheny River and through the national forest, where a scattering of private hunting and fishing "camps" are the only human presence. Watch for deer, and the occasional black bear, which pose a driving hazard.

At Pa. 59 proceed east through Warren to the
❸ Kinzua Dam and the **Allegheny Reservoir** *(814-726-0661. Visitor Center June-Aug. daily, Sept.-Oct. weekends)*, a popular boating, fishing, and picnicking spot with 91 miles of forested shoreline. Though authorized in 1936 to protect Pittsburgh and the Allegheny Valley downstream from floods, the dam wasn't begun until 1960, and it took five years to complete. Litigation and bickering between the federal government and the Seneca Indians—whose land and communities were flooded by the reservoir—raised tensions in the region for decades.

Farther east, turn north on Pa. 770 and US 219, then northeast on Pa. 346, Pa. 646, and N.Y. 16. As the drive crosses the border from Pennsylvania to New York, the forest and mountains give way to rolling farm country. A maze of immense quartz conglomerate boulders called

④ **Rock City Park** *(N.Y. 16, 5 miles S of Olean. 716-372-7790. May-Oct.; adm. fee)* sit in this border region. The rocks mark a prehistoric ocean floor, and visitors following the .75-mile nature trail will find themselves dwarfed among bold features with names like Balancing Rock and Indian Face.

West of Olean on N.Y. 17, you find the last wilderness recreation area on this trip. **Allegany State Park** *(State Park Rd., S of Salamanca. 716-354-9121. Adm. fee)* protects 65,000 acres of hiking, biking, and horseback riding trails, along with three campgrounds and a lake.

Another sanctuary, the Seneca's **Allegany Indian Reservation** surrounds most of the park. In the heart of the reservation, **Salamanca** boasts the **Seneca-Iroquois National Museum**★ *(Broad St. exit off N.Y. 17. 716-945-3133. Call for schedule; adm. fee)*, one of the mid-Atlantic's most engaging Native American museums. Using creative audio, video, and photo displays to highlight the collection of Seneca artifacts, the museum illuminates the nature of Indian life. Here you learn the Seneca's version of their fight to prevent the Allegheny Reservoir from flooding sacred lands.

Next door, a **Visitor Information Caboose** *(784 Broad*

Photo of Lucille Ball, Lucy-Desi Museum, Jamestown

St. 716-945-2034) is loaded with brochures and hard-to-find maps for upcoming sites, including the extensive Amish community in the Conewango Valley. Before leaving town, consider tanking up, because gas on the reservation is sold tax free.

Travelers craving a mountain resort experience will make a detour 9 miles north of Salamanca on US 219 to **⑤ Ellicottville** *(Chamber of Commerce 716-699-5046)*, a country town spruced up with restaurants, boutiques, and a brew pub. Crowds are drawn to the **Holiday Valley Resort** *(Holiday Valley Rd., off US 219. 716-699-2345)* for skiing, golf, swimming, the Jazz Festival *(mid-May)*, and the Summer Festival of the Arts *(early July)*.

Backtrack to N.Y. 17 and travel west, exiting at Randolph. From here, go north on N.Y. 241 and US 62 into the core of **Conewango Valley Amish country**★★ *(Visitor information 716-358-9701)*. Without the celebrity and hype that surrounds Pennsylvania Dutch country, the Amish farms around **Conewango** and **Leon** seem truly lost in the 18th century. Buggies rule the roads; thickly bearded farmers plow with horses; and locals make all kinds of goods—from furniture and quilts to cheese and candy. Small, hand-painted signs along country lanes announce these cottage industries, and respectful travelers (who don't take pictures) are welcome in the Amish shops *(closed Sun.)*.

The drive continues west on N.Y. 394 to **Jamestown** *(Chamber of Commerce 716-484-1101)*. Lucille Ball's hometown is still in love with her and for years has celebrated with a Lucy Fest. In 1996 the **Festival of New Comedy** *(In Sept., call chamber or museum for dates)* and the **Lucy-Desi Museum** *(212 Pine St. 716-484-7070. May-Sept. daily, Oct.-April weekends; adm. fee)* were launched. The museum displays over 500 of Lucy's personal possessions and shows video clips featuring Jamestown from the television series *I Love Lucy*. The town celebrates another famous native at the **Roger Tory Peterson Institute of Natural History** *(311 Curtis St. 716-665-2473. Closed Mon.; adm. fee)*, which offers the paintings of the famous artist and ornithologist, plus nature exhibits and a 27-acre wildlife sanctuary.

The famous arts and education center, the **⑥ Chautauqua Institution**★★ *(N.Y. 394. 716-357-6220 or 800-836-2787. Late June–Aug.; adm. fee)* awaits west of Jamestown on Chautauqua Lake. Begun in 1874 as a summer retreat for Sunday school teachers, the institution evolved into a premier summer resort that was especially fashionable around the turn of the century. Today it provides more than 140,000 guests with popular education combined with entertainment. They gather in the institution's hundreds of impeccably maintained Victorian buildings for lectures, concerts, opera, theater, and art exhibitions. At night, when the gingerbread buildings are sprinkled with lights and the symphony plays, Chautauqua attains a vintage atmosphere. There are a number of hotels and guest houses on the grounds.

If you think the Seneca Reservation, Amish country, and the Chautauqua Institution are sidesteps away from mainstream America, you might think you've entered a totally different dimension when you drive northeast on County Rd. 58 and N.Y. 60 to visit **Lily Dale Assembly**★ *(Dale Dr., off N.Y. 60 at Cassadaga Lakes. 716-595-8721. Late June–Aug.; adm. fee).* A lakeside community of Victorian cottages and public buildings, Lily Dale resembles a smaller, less prosperous version of the Chautauqua Institution. But free thinkers founded Lily Dale in 1879 as a reaction to Christian summer retreats such as Chautauqua. The community is dedicated to the science, philosophy, and religion of spiritualism. You can get a "reading" with a medium or attend lectures on psychic phenomena.

99

N.Y. 60 leads north to the Victorian town of **❼ Fredonia,** where guides to coastal vineyards and antique stores are available at the **Chamber of Commerce** *(5 E. Main St. 716-679-1565. Mon.-Fri.).* Then head back to Erie on N.Y. 5/Pa. 5—sometimes called the wine corridor—past vineyards carpeting the

Athenaeum Hotel, at the Chautauqua Institution

Lake Erie shoreline. The first grapevines were planted in the 1850s. Thanks to the rich soil and Lake Erie's moderating effects, the region has since flourished in wine-making. Among the several wineries open for tours and tastings are **Mazza Vineyards Winery** *(11815 E. Lake Rd./Pa. 5. 814-725-8695),* just across the Pennsylvania border, and **Penn Shore Winery** *(10225 E. Lake Rd./Pa. 5. 814-725-8688),* beyond the town of North East.

Laurel Highlands ★

● **430 miles** ● **4 days** ● **Spring through autumn**

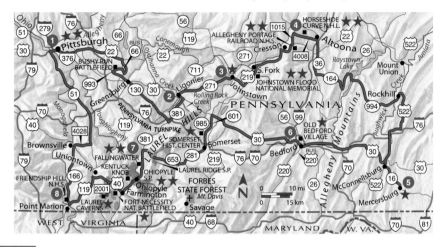

To tour the Laurel Highlands of southwestern Pennsylvania is to see how will and ingenuity combined with basic technology to turn a wilderness into a promised land…and, sometimes, a catastrophe. No region in America owes more to the development of canals, dams, railroads, mechanized mining, and blast furnaces.

Starting in Pittsburgh, this trip climbs east into the highlands to visit an Indian battleground and fort. At Johnstown, you learn about the nation's greatest dam disaster. From here, the route heads to the Allegheny Ridge and Horseshoe Curve, where the Pennsylvania Railroad Mainline, and the Pennsylvania Main Line Canal before it, crested the mountains. At the ridge's eastern slopes, the East Broad Top narrow-gauge railroad still survives from the days when mines exploited the mountains for coal, or "black gold." Frontier towns, valleys filled with mountain laurel—which gave the highlands their name—an architectural masterpiece, white-water rafting, Pennsylvania's largest cavern, and a Revolutionary-era fort, plantation, and castle are a few of the sights to see before returning to Pittsburgh.

The renaissance of ❶ **Pittsburgh★★** is no longer news, but the city's contemporary glitter still astonishes. Romantics ride the **Duquesne Incline★** *(1220 Grandview Ave. 412-381-1665. Fare)* and the **Monongahela Incline** *(Across from Station Square, E. Carson St. 412-442-2000. Fare)* for views of the city surrounded by rivers and green hills. Others favor the genteel paddlewheelers of **Gateway Clipper Fleet** *(9 Station Square Dock. 412-355-7980. Call for schedule; fare).*

Landlubbers begin at **Point State Park** *(Off Commonwealth Pl. 412-471-0235)*, where a 150-foot fountain signifies the meeting of the Allegheny, Monongahela, and Ohio Rivers. Then-Maj. George Washington sited the first fort on this strategic spot in 1753. A contested area in the French and Indian War, the point finally fell under British control in 1758. They named their new stronghold after the English Prime Minister William Pitt and developed the site as a frontier river port. The 1764 **Fort Pitt Blockhouse** *(412-471-1764. Wed.-Sun.)* is the only surviving structure, but signs point out what was there and a re-created bastion now houses the **Fort Pitt Museum** *(412-281-9284. Wed.-Sun.; adm. fee).*

Pittsburgh's main **Visitor Information Center** *(Liberty Ave., adj. to Gateway Center. 412-281-7711 or 800-366-0093. Closed Sun. Jan.-Feb.)* stands near the park's eastern border. Stop here, or at the satellite center *(closed Sun.)* near the top of the Monongahela Incline, on Grandview Avenue, to pick up maps and materials on attractions and such cultural events as symphony at **Heinz Hall** *(600 Penn Ave. 412-392-4900),* or theater at the **Benedum Center for the Performing Arts** *(7th and Penn Ave. 412-456-6666).*

For shopping, take the subway or walk across the Smithfield Street Bridge to **Station Square**★ *(Carson and Smithfield Sts.),* a former railroad station refurbished as an urban mall, complete with machine and railroad relics. The **Strip District** *(Penn. Ave., N of Civic Center)* is the place

Pittsburgh by night

Portrait by Peter Paul Rubens, Frick Art Museum

Robber Baron or Robin Hood?

102

In the minds of many, Andrew Carnegie (1835-1919), the self-educated Scottish immigrant who rose from textile bobbin boy to steel tycoon, is the epitome of the 19th-century "robber barons," who built their wealth on corruption and the backs of labor. But with an annual income of $50,000 by the age of 33, Carnegie made a personal vow: "Beyond this never earn— make no effort to increase fortune, but spend the surplus each year for benevolent [sic] purposes." During his life, Carnegie gave more than 325 million dollars to the "swimming one-tenth of society," funding over 2,500 libraries and the Peace Palace at The Hague.

to go for produce markets and trendy eateries. The new **Senator John Heinz Pittsburgh Regional History Center**★ *(1212 Smallman St. 412-454-6000. Adm. fee)* is here, too, keeping western Pennsylvania's history alive through videos and lively exhibits. Before leaving downtown, consider crossing the Allegheny River to the North Side, where the **Andy Warhol Museum**★ *(117 Sandusky St. 412-237-8300. Wed.-Sun.; adm. fee)* features 500 works by this native son and pop art legend.

To see the cultural institutions built by Andrew Carnegie, Henry Phipps, and Henry Clay Frick, wealthy industrialists who called this city their home, head to the Oakland section via the West Penn Parkway (I-376) and Forbes Avenue. Your landmark here is the 42-story Gothic **Cathedral of Learning**★ *(Forbes Ave. and Bigelow Blvd. 412-624-6000. Adm. fee)*, which contains classrooms in the style of 25 different cultures and marks the center of the **University of Pittsburgh** *(412-642-6000)*. Within a few blocks stands **Carnegie Mellon University** *(412-268-2102)* and a number of cultural attractions originally funded by Andrew Carnegie. Clustered across the street from the Cathedral of Learning stand a concert hall, a library, and the **Carnegie Museums of Pittsburgh**★★ *(4400 Forbes Ave. 412-622-3131. Closed Mon.; adm. fee)*, which offer exceptional collections of art and natural history, including Impressionist and Postimpressionist art, dinosaurs, and Egyptology.

Flower lovers won't miss the **Phipps Conservatory**★ *(412-622-6914. Closed Mon.; adm. fee)*, located within Schenley Park. Nearby, **Clayton** *(7227 Reynolds St. 412-371-0600. Closed Mon.; adm. fee. Reservations recommended in summer)*, the estate of Henry Clay Frick, is a popular stop for anyone interested in how the "robber barons" lived. Here, you will also find the **Frick Art Museum**★ *(412-371-0600. Closed Mon.)*, with a strong collection of European paintings and decorative arts.

Leaving Pittsburgh, take I-376 east to US 22. Follow this some 10 miles east through Murrysville to Pa. 66 *(toll)* south. At the Greensburg/Harrison City exit, turn onto Bus. Pa. 66 north to Pa. 993 west. After about 3 miles you will come to the quiet spaces of **Bushy Run Battlefield** *(Pa. 993. 412-527-5584. Wed.-Sun.; adm. fee)*. Site of a decisive battle in 1763 known as Pontiac's War, in which the British defeated the Indian offensive, the battlefield includes a Visitor Center *(April-Oct.)* and self-guided tours through woods and rolling hills.

Just west of the battlefield, take Pa. 130 east, then head

north on Pa. 381. The route winds through small towns, woods, and pastures, among the horse farms and châteaus of the **Rolling Rock Valley**★. In the restored Georgian town of ❷ **Ligonier,** stop by **Fort Ligonier**★ *(US 30 and Pa. 711. 412-238-9701. April-Oct.; adm. fee).* The log fortress originally built by the British to fight the French and Indian War has been reconstructed and brought to life with reenactments, encampments, and crafts people. Interpretive exhibits, decorative arts, and period rooms are on view in the museum.

Follow Pa. 711 and Pa. 271 over Laurel Hill and enter a different epoch in mountain conquest—the early industrial era—at ❸ **Johnstown**★ *(Convention & Visitors Bureau 814-536-7993 or 800-237-8590).* A steel town in the deep, narrow Conemaugh Valley, Johnstown is where some 2,200 people died when the South Fork Dam burst in 1889. It was one of the worst natural disasters in U.S. history. To grasp the devastation, start at the **Johnstown Flood Museum**★ *(304 Washington St. 814-539-1889 or 888-222-1889. Adm. fee),* inside the library Carnegie donated to the town after the flood. Powerful displays are supported by a relief map animated with sound and fiber optics to illustrate the day a 40-foot wall of water rushed down the valley, wiping out the town in 10 minutes. An Academy Award-winning documentary film shows hourly.

For a valley overview, ride up the **Johnstown Inclined Plane**★ *(711 Edgehill Dr. 814-536-1816. Fare),* built after the flood to provide an escape route to higher ground. Like the Pittsburgh versions but steeper, this incline also carries cars. At the top await a restaurant, sculpture park, observation deck, and, on weekend nights, a popular laser light show.

Fort Ligonier

From here, proceed north on US 219 to the **Johnstown Flood National Memorial**★★ *(Off US 219. 814-495-4643. Adm. fee).* Along the approach to the ruins of the South Fork Dam, signs tell you to tune your radio to a park broadcast detailing the events surrounding the catastrophe. You can drive around the banks of what was formerly Lake

Why Americans Don't Speak French

Up until the mid-18th century, English colonists controlled only the Atlantic coast of America, while the French claimed much of the continental interior. The French and Indian War ignited in 1754 when the French moved south, and the British tried to move west. The action centered near Pittsburgh, when the French drove the English from Fort Prince George and replaced it with Fort Duquesne. A young George Washington was sent to dislodge the French; and faced his only surrender and first defeat, at Fort Necessity. The war turned in 1758, when British Prime Minister William Pitt engineered a French defeat. The 1763 Treaty of Paris yielded all French territory east of the Mississippi, plus Spanish lands in Florida, to English control.

Conemaugh, and wonder at the negligence that permitted an ill-repaired dam to maintain this watery playground for wealthy industrialists. Their summer cottages and South Fork Fishing and Hunting Club still line the shore. At the Visitor Center, models, exhibits, and a 35-minute film, *Black Friday,* tell the story of how the dam burst under the pressure of torrential rains.

The drive continues uphill on US 219 and US 22 to the summit of Cresson Mountain, where signs lead to the **Allegheny Portage Railroad National Historic Site**★★ *(Off US 22. 814-886-6150. Adm. fee).* This crest stands atop the Allegheny Ridge, which loomed as a 1,200-foot-high barrier to American expansion in the early 19th century. Spurred by the success of the Erie Canal and railroad technology, Pennsylvania engineers began digging the Pennsylvania Main Line Canal to connect Philadelphia and Pittsburgh. To conquer the ridge, builders devised a series of 10 railroad-like incline planes to portage the canal boats, broken in sections, with cars attached to thick ropes moved up and down the tracks by stationary steam engines. The park features a Visitor Center with a film, full-scale locomotive, and informative exhibits. A series of interpretive walks lead to Incline Number 6, Skew Arch Bridge, an engine house, a quarry, and the Lemon House tavern. Costumed interpreters unveil canal and portage railroad life, and the summer bustles with evenings of concerts and lectures.

From here, follow signs north on Pa. 1015 and Pa. 4008 to nearby ❹ **Horseshoe Curve National Historic Landmark**★★ *(Pa. 4008. 814-946-0834. Closed Mon. late Oct.–mid-April; adm. fee).* An engineering marvel, the nearly symmetrical railroad curve opened in 1854 to enable trains to mount the Allegheny Ridge. Visitor Center exhibits detail the history and engineering of the curve and the rail line that put the canal out of business. Watch while as many as 50 trains a day traverse the curve, using convoys of "helper engines" on the uphill climb and filling the air with brake smoke going down.

East of the curve via Pa. 4008 lies **Altoona** *(Visitor Center 814-943-4183 or 800-842-5866),* the town the

Old log house, Bedford Village

Along Pa. 281

Pennsylvania Railroad, now Conrail, founded in 1849 as its major construction and repair stop. Thousands of steam locomotives were built here, and you can see examples and learn the story of the once mighty railroad at the **Altoona Railroader's Memorial Museum**★ *(9th Ave. near Station Mall. Moving to adj. Master Mechanics Building in 1998. 814-946-0834. Closed Mon.; adm. fee).*

The high point for rail fans on this trip comes after circling southeast from Altoona through the Appalachian's eastern slopes on Pa. 36, Pa. 164, Pa. 26, and Pa. 994 to **Rockhill** and the **East Broad Top Railroad National Historic Monument**★★ *(US 522. 814-447-3011. June–late Oct. Sat.-Sun.; fare).* The 3-foot gauge East Broad Top dates from the 1870s, when it began to haul coal and passengers through the Aughwick Valley. The railroad closed in 1956, but the steam locomotives, cars, tracks, yards, and shops survived until preservationists resurrected 10 miles of the track and facilities for rides and exploration. The **Rockhill Trolley Museum** *(814-447-9576. Late May–Oct. Sat.-Sun.; adm. fee)* adjoins the rail yard.

Join US 522 south to McConnellsburg and continue south along Pa. 16 into the village of ❺ **Mercersburg**★ *(Chamber of Commerce 717-485-4064).* The quiet streets of this early 19th-century settlement recall the days when America's 15th President, James Buchanan, grew up nearby and launched his Presidential campaign from the Mansion House Hotel on the square. Buchanan's birthplace, a 1791 furnished log cabin, still stands on the

Laurel Highlands

Laurel Highlands Trail at Laurel Ridge State Park, off Pa. 653

Time Machines

The rugged Allegheny Ridge served as an immense barrier to early-day travelers wanting to journey from Philadelphia to Pittsburgh. The arduous trip took about 21 days on horseback. In the 1800s, boats along the Pennsylvania Main Line Canal—with the added help of the Allegheny Portage Railroad—reduced the trip to four days. Then, with the opening of the Horseshoe Curve in 1834, the Pennsylvania Railroad traveled across the state in 13 hours. Today along the interstate, you can leave Philadelphia after breakfast and be in Pittsburgh in time for lunch.

grounds of the **Mercersburg Academy** (*300 E. Seminary St. 717-328-6173*). The buildings of this independent secondary school cluster around a Gothic chapel, whose 49-bell carillon rings out on Sundays at 3 p.m. (*Sept.-May*).

Backtrack on Pa. 16 and head west on US 30, back into the mountains. Originally called Forbes Road for British Gen. John Forbes, who cut a path through the wilderness to reclaim Pittsburgh's Point from the French in 1758, the trail served as the major pioneer route before the canal and railroad eras. Revisit those times at ❻**Old Bedford Village**★ (*Bus. US 220, Bedford. 814-623-1156 or 800-238-4347. May-Oct.; adm. fee*). A reproduction of a frontier community, the village includes 40 log houses, shops, and public buildings. Interpreters demonstrate crafts and highlight the days when Bedford saw action in the French and Indian War, fell to colonial rebels during the Revolution, and drew President George Washington and Federal troops here to quell the Whiskey Rebellion.

Farther west on US 30 and south on Pa. 601 lies another historic village, the **Somerset Historical Center** (*Pa. 601 and Pa. 985, N of Somerset. 814-445-6077. Call for hours; adm. fee*). It offers a short film about the mountain frontier, a guided tour that takes in a log house, and a covered bridge and maple sugar camp.

Travel southwest from Somerset on Pa. 281 and Pa. 653, and south on Pa. 381, where the steep terrain and crisp air hint that you are near **Mount Davis,** the state's highest point, at 3,213 feet. Architect Frank Lloyd Wright captured the drama of the region's terrain in his 1936 masterpiece, ❼ **Fallingwater**★★ (*Pa. 381, N of Ohiopyle. 412-329-8501. Tues.-Sun. April–mid-Nov., weekends only mid-Nov.–Dec. and March; adm. fee. Reservations advised*). Called the "best all-time work of American architecture," the house employs local stone, poured concrete, glass walls, and cantilever construction to blend with the wooded hillside, and thrust above the waterfalls of Bear Run.

Continue south on Pa. 381 into the village of **Ohiopyle,** the name of which may derive from a Native American word meaning "white, frothy water." This is an apt description for the roiling waters of the **Youghiogheny River.** Outfitters in the village and **Ohiopyle**

State Park★★ *(412-329-8591)* are the
places to go for a white-water rafting
experience through the 1,700-foot-deep
gorge. The 19,046-acre park also features hiking, biking, camping, fishing,
and hunting areas with vistas on the
falls and rapids of the "Yough" (YOCK).

Rafting the Youghiogheny

Another fine Frank Lloyd Wright
house, **Kentuck Knob** *(Off Pa. 381.
412-329-1901. April-Nov. Tues.-Sun.,
and by appt.; adm. fee)* stands nearby
and offers tours. Then proceed south on Pa.
381 and west on US 40 to explore the wooden stockade
of **Fort Necessity National Battlefield**★ *(US 40, Farm-
ington. 412-329-5512. Adm. fee),* where young George
Washington staged the first major confrontation of the
French and Indian War, in 1754.

Just a few miles away, **Laurel Caverns**★ *(Off US 40.
412-438-3003. Daily May-Oct., weekends only March-April and
Nov.; adm. fee),* Pennsylvania's largest cave attraction, features almost 3 miles of passages and rooms with names
such as the Hall of the Mountain King.

Go farther west on US 40 and US 119. At Point Marion,
turn north on Pa. 166 and follow the Monongahela River
past two estates that figured in the conquest of the Laurel
Highlands. The first, ❽ **Friendship Hill National Historic Site** *(Pa. 166. 412-329-9190),* centers on a house
begun in 1789 by Albert
Gallatin, who served infant
America in finance and
politics. The brick-and-
stone mansion stands on a
bluff above the Mononga-
hela River, surrounded by
fields, woods, and trails.

North on Pa. 166, and
briefly west on US 40, in
Brownsville, is **Nemacolin
Castle** *(Bet. Front and Bras-
hear Sts. 412-785-6882. Tues.-
Sun. June-Aug., weekends in
spring and fall; adm. fee),*
home of Jacob Bowman, a
trader who came to this area in 1789. The mansion's 22
furnished rooms reflect life in America from colonial
times to the late Victorian era. Now follow Pa. 4028 to Pa.
51, which leads back to Pittsburgh.

Frank Lloyd Wright's Fallingwater

Bucktail Wilderness

● **320 miles** ● **3 to 4 days** ● **Spring through autumn**

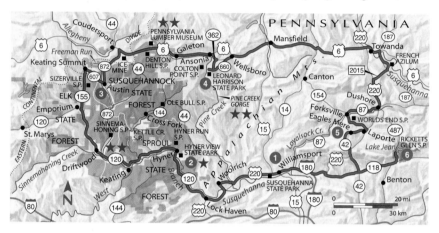

You can get literally and figuratively lost on this long loop around north-central Pennsylvania's state forests in the Appalachian Mountains. This is a trip for those who lust after mountain scenery—with lots of camping, fishing, and hiking opportunities, the attractions are largely natural or related to the once-thriving timber industry.

The trip begins in Williamsport, a town that grew rich on lumbering, and is now the home of the Little League World Series and museum. The route grows wild as it travels through state forests and parks along the West Branch Susquehanna River and its tributaries, to the ruins of a historic dam disaster. Next the road traverses high country, with stops at an excellent lumber museum, a ski area, the "Grand Canyon" of Pennsylvania, and the civilized town of Wellsboro. Circling back to Williamsport, the drive passes two of Pennsylvania's most spectacular and lesser-known state parks—Worlds End and Ricketts Glen.

Known affectionately as "Billtown" to its citizens,
❶ **Williamsport** *(Chamber of Commerce 717-326-1971 or 800-358-9900)* offers unexpected lures to visitors. Take the Maynard Street exit off I-180 and enter this city of 32,000 along West Fourth Street, also known as **Millionaires' Row.** Here the handsome Victorian mansions amid towering shade trees offer strong indications of the prosperity that infused this region during the 19th century, when lumber was king and Williamsport's location on the West Branch Susquehanna River made it a busy shipping center.

Sitting among these mansions, the **Lycoming County Historical Society Museum** *(858 W. Fourth St. 717-326-3326. May-Oct. Tues.-Sun., Nov.-April Tues.-Sat.; adm. fee)* offers more than 35 exhibits, many unfolding the story of the white pine and hemlock lumbering that nearly stripped the nearby forests a hundred years ago.

For effortless historic sightseeing, catch a ride on the **Herdic Trolley** *(Pickup at Sheraton Williamsport Inn, 100 Pine St. 717-326-2500 or 800-248-9287. Mid-June–Aug. Tues., Thurs., and Sat.; fare),* or the sternwheel riverboat ***Hiawatha*** *(Arch St. in Susquehanna State Park. 717-326-1221 or 800-358-9900. Tues.-Sun. June-Aug., Sat.-Sun. May and Sept.-Oct.; fare).* The 18th-century **Thomas Lightfoot Inn** *(2887 S. Reach Rd. 717-326-6396),* once a station on the underground railway, now features distinctive meals and lodging.

Little League baseball began in Williamsport in 1939 with three teams, and the Little League World Series is held here each August. The interpretive displays and memorabilia at the **Little League Museum** *(US 15. 717-326-3607. Adm. fee)* tell the story of the league's development. Visitors can participate in batting and pitching areas.

Next, take US 220 west to the exit for **Woolrich,** named after the famous outerwear company and home to the original **Woolrich Store** *(Park Ave. 717-769-7401),* offering big discounts. While you're bargain-hunting, check out **Bald Eagle Factory Outlets** *(1 Outlet Ln. 717-769-0550),* a mall with 30 vendors that has sprouted nearby.

A few miles farther west, **Lock Haven** *(Visitor Center 717-748-5782)* offers another cultural oasis on the edge of

the Big Woods, as this area of north-central Pennsylvania is known. Home to **Lock Haven University** *(717-893-2027),* this college town also features **Water Street** *(Walking tour maps available at Ross Library, 232 W. Main St. 717-748-3321. Mon.-Sat.),* which is on the National Register of Historic Places; the houses here represent 33 architectural styles. One, the Victorian **Heisey Museum** *(362 Water St. 717-748-7254.*

Little League Museum, Williamsport

Tues.-Fri. and second Sun. of month; donation) is filled with memorabilia from the region's prosperous logging days.

In summer, enjoy a show at the nearby **Millbrook Playhouse** *(Off US 220, Mill Hall. 717-748-8083. June-Aug.; adm. fee).* Or drive out to the town's newest attraction, the

Bucktail Wilderness

Piper Aviation Museum ★ *(W. D. Piper Memorial Airport. 717-748-8283. Donation),* located in the engineering building at the former Piper Aircraft plant.

Flood ruins, Austin Dam Disaster

Before leaving Lock Haven, stop at Clinton County's **Tourism Promotion Agency** *(Court House Annex, 151 Susquehanna Ave. 717-893-4037)* to pick up maps and brochures for the state forests, parks, campgrounds, trails, and recreational waterways ahead. Then follow scenic **Pa. 120** ★★ north for 75 miles along the West Branch Susquehanna and Sinnemahoning Creek, one of the prettiest drives in the mid-Atlantic.

It begins as an uphill meander between the sparkling West Branch and steep, forested valleys, climbing toward the Appalachian Plateau and the eastern Continental Divide near Coudersport. Logged nearly bare during the late 19th and early 20th centuries by timber companies in search of prize hemlocks, white pines, and hardwoods, nearly 750,000 acres of this wilderness now constitute the **Sproul, Elk,** and **Susquehannock State Forests.** Today, the maturing forest is a habitat for white-tailed deer, black bear, elk, and wild turkey (the entire route is so thick with deer that they often halt traffic).

Pine Creek Gorge, Pennsylvania's "Grand Canyon"

Most of the valley along Pa. 120 (between Lock Haven and Emporium) constitutes **Bucktail State Park Natural Area.** Designated as a "legislative" park, it is really a scenic drive on undeveloped state land. There are no facilities, but the surroundings are an unspoiled mix of hills, valleys, and rushing water. Most of the year traffic is light, but during fall leaf-peeping weekends the road can get packed. The most dramatic time to visit is during the spring runoff, when the streams swell with ice and melting snow. Stop and take in the view from the railroad bridge at **Keating,** where the West Branch and Sinnemahoning Creek meet. From here it is easy to picture the event that gave the park its name: On April 27, 1861, a gang of mountainmen built rafts at Driftwood to ride the cresting Susquehanna south to fight in the Civil War; one raft bore a buck tail on its masthead, earning the men their regimental nickname.

Just a half hour's drive from Lock Haven, ❷ **Hyner View State Park**★ *(Follow signs from Pa. 120 in Hyner. 717-923-6000)* makes a good perch for a picnic with a glorious view of the river valley. When the weather is fair, you'll probably see hang-glider pilots strapping into their colorful wings and launching from the escarpment. Campsites are available at nearby **Hyner Run State Park** *(717-923-6000)* or slightly farther away at the **Kettle Creek, Ole Bull, Sinnemahoning,** and **Sizerville State Parks** *(State park information 717-783-0139 or 800-63-PARKS).*

North of Emporium, follow Pa. 155 and Pa. 607 to the hamlet of ❸ **Austin** *(Visitor Center 814-546-2665),* today a village of 590 people. You won't immediately see many signs of the catastrophe that wiped out the logging boom town of about 3,000 people here on September 30, 1911. But by following Pa. 872 north along Freeman Run, you will soon spy the extensive ruins of the Bayless Pulp & Paper Mill, agent and victim of the dam break and site of the **Austin Dam Disaster**★★ *(Pa. 872).* Farther up the road, the concrete dam stands tall but sprung open like a door. Built to supply the pulp mill with a constant flow of water, the poorly designed dam gave way under pressure from torrential rains, releasing a flood that roared down the hollow like a great white cloud and left at least 80 dead. Treasure hunters claim that a trove of gold, silver, and jewelry lies scattered over the flatlands south of town.

Just before reaching Coudersport, the retreat of Eliot Ness after his mob-busting days, Pa. 872 crests the eastern Continental Divide separating the Susquehanna and the Allegheny watersheds. East of town off US 6 and Pa. 44, sits the nearly hundred-year-old tourist attraction, the **Ice**

Eternal Tap

Long before microbreweries were in vogue, tiny **Straub Brewery** *(303 Sorg St. 814-834-2875. Mon.-Fri.)* in the town of St. Marys *(Pa. 120, W of Emporium)* was producing a no additives, no preservatives, no syrups brew that connoisseurs rank with the best beers in the world. Their hospitality room, "The Eternal Tap," lets visitors of legal age, with a designated driver, come in and drink for free without taking a tour, endearing itself to beer aficionados. When a traveler asked a local mountain man about the brewery, the native shook his head in ignorance: "I've tried to see what's going on in there a dozen times, but I just never get past that fountain they got right inside the front door."

111

Bucktail Wilderness

French Azilum, near Towanda

Snake Mania

Potter County's **Cross Fork** (Pa. 144. 717-923-1428) goes wild for serpents during the annual snake hunt weekend in late June. Scores of snake hunters register here to scour the woods for plentiful snakes—mostly rattlers. While the hunters are looking for the big one, families compete in non-poisonous snake sacking contests to raise adrenaline levels among the crowd. Everyone gets pumped up for the reappearance of the hunters, who measure and show off catches of 4-foot vipers. The finale comes with rounds of snake-sacking competitions in which teams of two adults try bagging five rattlers in record time to win the State Championship—without getting bitten.

Mine *(Ice Mine Rd. June-Aug.; adm. fee)*. This cavern's claim to fame is its logic-defying ability to make ice in the summer, but its charm rests in its old-time roadside-attraction ambience. You can jaw about local history and strange goings on in Potter County with the proprietor for hours.

Driving east along US 6, the mountain and trails of **Ski Denton** *(814-435-2115)* rise on your right, part of Denton Hill State Park. On your left the **Pennsylvania Lumber Museum** ★ ★ *(814-435-2652. April-Nov.; adm. fee)* offers exhibits explaining the history of local logging, and a re-created lumber camp that includes a sawmill, workers' quarters, a mess hall, shops, and an engine house and railway, with a 1912 Shay locomotive and logging cars.

The high country's biggest attraction lies just south of Ansonia on Pa. 660; **Pine Creek Gorge** ★ ★ *(Off US 6 and Pa. 362)*, known as the "Grand Canyon" of Pennsylvania. Bordered by ❹ **Leonard Harrison** and **Colton Point State Parks,** the canyon is 50 miles long and 1,000 feet deep. For insights in the geology, geography, and attractions, stop at the **Visitor Center** *(Pa. 660. 717-724-3061. Mid-May–mid-Oct. Sat.-Sun., call for other hours)* in Harrison State Park. There's a good view up and down the canyon from here, and you can follow the **Turkey Path Trail** a mile to the bottom. You can also ask about the new bike trail along the canyon's base. The area has a good selection of guide services, including **Pine Creek Outfitters** *(US 6, Ansonia. 717-724-3003)*, which provide everything for rafting and canoeing expeditions.

After a few days in the wilds, the gaslit streets, village green, and well-kept houses of **Wellsboro** *(Chamber of Commerce 114 Main St. 717-724-1926)*, east on US 6, can look very welcoming. There are specialty and antique shops, restored mansions, a historic walking tour *(maps available at Chamber of Commerce and Tioga museum)*, the small **Tioga County Historical Society's Robinson House Museum** *(120 Main St. 717-724-6116. Mon.-Fri.)*, and a few convenient motels and B&Bs. Nothing is very fancy, but you're sure to enjoy the fare at the art deco **Wellsboro Diner** *(19 Main St. 717-724-3992)*, or aboard the dining car of the **Tioga Central Railroad** *(Pa. 287, 3 miles N of Wellsboro. 717-724-0990. Early May–late Oct. Sat.-Sun.; fare)*.

East of Wellsboro, the route traverses dairy country before veering south on US 220 into a region that lives up to its Seneca Indian name—the **Endless Mountains.** Although no museum is dedicated to the composer of "Camptown Races," Stephen Foster's ebullient spirit infuses the mountains near his boyhood home in

Towanda *(Chamber of Commerce 717-268-2732)* on the East Branch Susquehanna. Outside of town, Pa. 187 south leads to the **French Azilum** *(Pa. 2014. 717-265-3376. Mem. Day–Labor Day Wed.-Sun., May and Sept. weekends; adm. fee),* or "asylum." In 1793 French noblemen fleeing the revolution found refuge in this serene valley. Today, log cabins filled with historical exhibits detail their years here.

113

You can lose your sense of time following Pa. 2015, US 220, Pa. 87, and Pa. 154 through the twisting hemlock valley of Loyalsock Creek. After passing the old-time fairgrounds and covered bridge in **Forksville,** discover **Worlds End State Park** *(Pa. 154. 717-924-3287).* Built around an "S" curve in the creek, the park attracts campers, hikers, and kayakers, whose laughter at the swimming hole echoes like banjo music.

Nearby on Pa. 42, ❺ **Eagles Mere** has a very different "campground" feel. Begun in the mid-19th century as a Chautauqua-style

Ricketts Glen State Park

summer retreat around a mountain lake, Eagles Mere evolved into an exclusive summer resort for Philadelphians. The community of large, "stick Victorian" summer cottages still retains a privileged feel, but four lodges, including the **Eagles Mere Inn** *(Mary Ave. 717-525-3273),* welcome guests.

Continue south on Pa. 42 and pick up Pa. 118 east to ❻ **Ricketts Glen State Park** *(Pa. 487, Benton. 717-477-5675).* Five-hundred-year-old giant pines, hemlocks, and oaks shade two deep gorges in the park with more than 20 named waterfalls. **Lake Jean** has a long beach and plentiful fishing *(license required),* where you can dream away days in the sun before heading back to Williamsport.

Pennsylvania Dutch Country

● 195 miles ● 3 days ● Spring and autumn

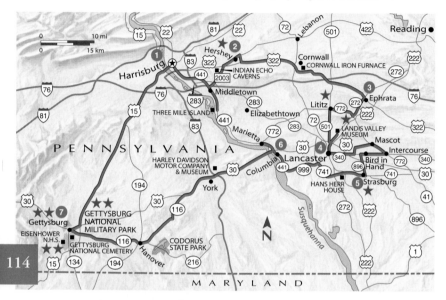

At the core of Pennsylvania Dutch life lies a passion for hard work and self-reliance, qualities evident on a visit to the state capital of Harrisburg. The route then heads east to Hershey, a company town turned family amusement center. Next, tour the Lebanon Valley's prosperous farms and historic ironmaking communities, and the Lancaster area's country villages, where Amish farm families travel by horse-and-buggy and steam railroading endures. The drive lingers among 19th-century port towns before crossing the Susquehanna River to haunting Gettysburg.

Today, proud residents of ❶ **Harrisburg** *(Office of the Mayor 717-255-3040)* point to the city's rebound from the ravages of urban decay, offering visitors a variety of interesting sites all within walking distance. The city's focal point is the **State Capitol** *(N. 3rd and State Sts. 717-787-6810 or 800-868-7672)*, which offers daily tours. Teddy Roosevelt called the Renaissance-style capitol "the handsomest building I ever saw," and you might well agree after seeing the stained glass, chandeliers, antique clocks, the dome modeled after St. Peter's Basilica in Vatican City, and the marble staircase and surrounding balconies drawn from those

State Capitol, Harrisburg

in the old Paris Opera House. The **Welcome Center** *(Mon.-Fri.)* in the East Wing can help provide a brief overview of Pennsylvania history and politics.

Before taking to the streets, stroll the parks of the **Capitol Complex** and peruse the many exhibits at the **State Museum of Pennsylvania** *(N. 3rd and North Sts. 717-787-4978. Closed Mon.)*. You can't miss Peter F. Rothermel's huge *Battle of Gettysburg, Pickett's Charge,* one of the world's largest framed paintings.

As you head south to the business district, check out **Strawberry Square** *(Third and Market Sts.),* an indoor mall combining reclaimed historic buildings with new construction to host more than 80 specialty shops, galleries, and ethnic restaurants. The **Museum of Scientific Discovery** *(717-233-7969. Closed Mon.; adm. fee),* part of this complex, brims with hands-on exhibits and demonstrations.

Continue west toward the Susquehanna River past **Governor's Row** *(N. Front St. bet. Walnut and Strawberry Sts.),* a collection of early 19th-century town houses built for the state's early leaders. One, home to William Finely when he was governor (1817-1821), now houses the art school, studios, and galleries of the **Art Association of Harrisburg** *(21 N. Front St. 717-236-1432);* two floors of rotating national and regional works include sculpture, painting, graphics, and photography.

If you are in search of a fresh breeze, stroll across the street to **Riverfront Park** and its 5 miles of green space. Or cross Walnut Street Bridge *(bikes and pedestrians only)* to 63-acre **City Island.** Since its development in 1987, the island has been the city's most popular venue, drawing people to its beach, three marinas, minor league baseball stadium, and more. You can also choose your mode of island transport—by carriage, on horseback, behind a miniature steam train, or on the ***Pride of the Susquehanna*** *(E end of island. 717-234-6500. May-Oct. Tues.-Sun.; fare)* for a narrated cruise aboard a stern-driven paddlewheeler.

Just east of Harrisburg in **Middletown,** you can board the **Middletown & Hummelstown Railroad** *(136 Brown St. 717-944-4435. Call for schedule; fare)* for a ride along the Union Canal to **Indian Echo Caverns** *(Off US 322 and Pa. 2003. Weather permitting; adm. fee),* where hermit William Wilson lived for 19 years.

About 10 miles south of Harrisburg looms **Three Mile Island** *(Visitor Center, Pa. 441. 717-948-8829. Mem. Day–Labor Day Thurs.-Sun., Thurs.-Sat. rest of year. Tour reservations required).* The Visitor Center, outside of the nuclear power plant, offers exhibits on this infamous facility, best known

Pennsylvania Deutsch

Pennsylvania "Dutch" ancestors did not come from Holland. The term "Dutch" is a corruption of Deutsch—German. Hearing news of William Penn's "noble experiment" in the 18th century, German families from throughout central Europe began coming to south-central Pennsylvania's rich farming valleys, seeking freedom to practice their Anabaptist faith. The various related "Dutch" groups include the Amish, Mennonites, and Moravians. To different degrees, they all practice intense spirituality, work at traditional trades such as farming or crafting, and hold onto their German roots. Old Order Amish reject the "outside world," with its flush toilets, cars, and electronics. Most Amish speak English in school, a German dialect among themselves, and High German at worship services. Nonviolence is a way of life.

115

Street signs, Hershey

Sweet Deal

More than a chocolate magnate, Milton S. Hershey was also a generous humanitarian. In 1909 he and his wife, Catherine, began the **Milton Hershey School** *(Governor Rd./Pa. 322, Hershey. 717-50-2000)*, a school for orphan boys. Quietly he endowed and expanded the facility to cover the education, medical costs, food, clothing, and shelter for more than 1,000 disadvantaged students per year. The school continues to be funded by Hershey's three-billion-dollars worth of trust and profits from the Hershey Companies. On campus, **Founders Hall** serves as a memorial to the school's benefactors, with a self-guided tour and short film highlighting the school's history.

for its partial meltdown in 1979. The Visitor Center offers dramatic views of the four cooling towers.

For a more lighthearted destination, head east along US 322 to ❷ **Hershey**★ *(Tourism and Convention Bureau 717-232-1377 or 800-995-0969)*. When Milton Hershey started the town in 1903, he pictured a community built by and for his employees. Today, Hershey is not only the capital of a chocolate empire, but also home of the Pennsylvania State University Medical Center...and probably the state's biggest tourist attraction west of Philadelphia. Notice the chocolate-kiss shaped street lights on your way to the **Hershey's Chocolate World and Visitor Center**★ *(Hersheypark Dr. and Park Blvd. 717-534-4900)*, where you can take a 12-minute automated ride among exhibits showing the chocolate-making process. Then walk to the nearby **Hershey Museum** *(170 W. Hersheypark Dr. 717-534-3439. Adm. fee)*, where displays chronicle the local Pennsylvania Dutch culture as well as the story of self-reliance behind Milton Hershey's accomplishments and his model town (see sidebar this page).

Conventioneers line up next to families to test drive world-class roller-coasters and other attractions at popular **Hersheypark**★ *(100 W. Hersheypark Dr. 717-534-3005 or 800-HERSHEY. Mem. Day–Labor Day, call for off-season hours; adm. fee)*, originally established as a recreation area for Hershey's workers. Opposite the park, **ZooAmerica North American Wildlife Park** *(Park Ave. 717-534-3860. Adm. fee)* presents animals and plants from five different regions of the United States. The "Gentle Woodlands" section does a good job showing deer, turkeys, raccoons, bobcats, and other animals that populate this region's wilderness. Finally, at **Hershey Gardens**★ *(Hotel Rd. 717-534-3492. Mid-May–Oct.; adm. fee)* await more than 8,000 roses in season.

Heading east, US 322 carries you into the farms of the Lebanon Valley. Colonists discovered iron ore in the hills of **Cornwall** in the 1730s, which were mined until 1972. The **Cornwall Iron Furnace** *(Follow signs from US 322. 717-272-9711. Closed Mon.; adm. fee)*, built into the side of a hill so that the ore, limestone, and charcoal could be poured into the furnace from the top, is the heart of the iron-making plantation that includes the restored furnace, shops, an open pit mine, and the ironmaster's house.

From Cornwall, the route zigzags through the land of the "Plain People," Pennsylvania Dutch who eschew many modern ways and dress in plain-colored weaves. To get a sense of the early history of German

immigration, follow US 322 east to
❸ **Ephrata** and the **Ephrata Cloister** ★
(632 W. Main St. 717-733-6600. Adm. fee),
one of the country's most successful
religious communities from 1732 to the
early 1800s. Medieval-style buildings
that housed the monastic commune still
stand. Known for its music, the cloister
was also an early center for printing
and publishing.

Central Market, Lancaster

To the west lies **Lititz** ★, a well-kept
town named for the Bohemia home of Moravian settlers
who came here in 1742. Step into the **Johannes Mueller
House** and the **Lititz Museum** *(145 E. Main St. 717-627-
4636. Mem. Day–Oct. Mon.-Sat.; adm. fee)* to pick up a self-
guided tour map and learn more about this settlement,
entirely church-owned until 1855. Across the street stands
Linden Hall, a girl's school dating back to 1746.

Watch workers dipping chocolate at the **Wilbur
Chocolate Candy Store and Americana Museum** *(48 N.
Broad St. 717-626-3249. Mon.-Sat.)* and twist your own soft
pretzels at the **Sturgis Bretzel House** *(219 E. Main St. 717-
626-4354. Closed Sun.; adm. fee).* Map lovers will want to
trace their travels on antique maps at the **Heritage Map
Museum** *(55 N. Water St. 717-626-5002. Closed Sun.; adm. fee).*

Drive south on Pa. 501, veering left onto Valley Road
and following signs to the **Landis Valley Museum** ★

117

Lancaster County farmland

(2451 Kissel Hill Rd. 717-569-0401. March–Dec. Tues.-Sun.; adm. fee). Here you can immerse yourself in the rural lifestyles of the German (or *Deutsch*) immigrants who came to be known as the Pennsylvania Dutch. This collection of buildings on 16 acres hosts crafts people and interpreters on three farmsteads, depicting life from the 1760s to the early 1900s.

As you approach Lancaster, watch for the Amish horse-and-buggies—and slow down. You may actually enjoy traveling at this pace. An essential stop, if only to grab the helpful map, is the **Pennsylvania Dutch Convention and Visitors Bureau** *(Just off US 30 bypass E of Lancaster, at 501 Greenfield Rd. 717-299-8901 or 800-PA-DUTCH).* You also might consult with the staff about staying in a B&B on one of a score of working farms. Remember: Anything that says it's "Amish" is not; Plain People do not capitalize on their religion. Get advice about the area attractions and pick a few that suit your interests.

Once in ❹ **Lancaster,** you can learn more about the region's settlers at the **Heritage Center Museum of Lancaster County** *(Penn Sq. 717-299-6440. April-Dec. Tues.-Sat.; donation).* Housed in the old city hall, it features decorative arts from the 18th and 19th centuries. Nearby **Central Market** *(Penn. Sq. 717-291-4739. Tues., Fri., Sat.)*—one of the country's oldest enclosed markets—is a great place to stock up on vegetables, fresh fruits, meats, and flowers.

A short drive away stands the elegant, federal-style **Wheatland** *(1120 Marietta Ave. 717-392-8721. April-Nov.; adm. fee),* purchased in 1848 by then Secretary of State James Buchanan, who went on to become the nation's only bachelor President. It contains original furnishings, including gifts from foreign countries.

Strasburg Rail Road locomotive

Then shun the highways and enter the Amish countryside by driving, slowly, east of Lancaster on Pa. 340. Turn left on Horseshoe Road, right on Mount Sidney Road, then left onto Stumptown Road. Wandering among Amish farms, look for neatly lettered signs proclaiming "quilts," "furniture," or "baked goods." If you are respectful and refrain from snapping pictures, you might find a treasure, and you will certainly connect with gentle people.

At the junction of Stumptown Road and Pa. 772 stands **Mascot Mill**★★ *(717-656-9214. May-Oct. Mon.-Sat.).* Built in

1760, it is one of the gems of the area, and a free tour documents the evolution of the rural milling industry. Next, be sure to visit the **People's Place**★★ *(3513 Main St., Intercourse. 717-768-7171. Mon.-Sat.; adm. fee),* where you'll gain an in-depth understanding of Amish and Mennonite life through sensitive exhibits and a three-screen, 30-minute documentary film.

Golden Plough Tavern, York

At Intercourse, bear west on Pa. 340 through farm country and the pleasant town of Bird in Hand to Pa. 896, which leads south to ❺ **Strasburg**★ *(Visitor Center 717-687-7922).* The **Strasburg Rail Road Company**★ *(Pa. 741. 717-687-7522. April-Oct., call for off-season hours; fare)* runs 45-minute trips through Amish farmland to the village of Paradise. But before you ride, cross the road to the **Railroad Museum of Pennsylvania**★ *(717-687-8628. Closed Mon. Nov.-April; adm. fee)* to view more than 70 cars and locomotives. If you crave still more trains, visit the five layouts at the nearby **National Toy Train Museum** *(Off Pa. 741. 717-687-8976. Daily May-Oct., weekends only April and Nov.-Dec.; adm. fee).*

Farther west, off Pa. 741, you'll find the **Hans Herr House** *(Hans Herr Rd. 717-464-4438. April-Nov. Mon.-Sat.; adm. fee).* Built in 1719 and beautifully restored, it is the oldest house in Lancaster County and the nation's oldest Mennonite meetinghouse. It figures in several paintings by Andrew Wyeth, a descendent of the original builder.

Your rural drive moves toward the Susquehanna River via Pa. 741, Pa. 999, and Pa. 441 to ❻ **Columbia** and **The Watch and Clock Museum** *(514 Poplar St. 717-684-8261. May-Sept. Tues.-Sun., Oct.-April Tues.-Sat.; adm. fee).* Here 8,000 items trace the history of timekeeping since the 1600s. The **Wright's Ferry Mansion** *(2nd and Cherry Sts. 717-684-4325. May-Oct. Tues.-Wed. and Fri.-Sat.; adm. fee)* re-creates 18th-century Quaker life and includes a great collection of English needlework and Pennsylvania furniture before 1750. A few miles north, **Marietta** *(Chamber of Commerce 717-684-5249)* is a haven for strollers in a town where almost half of the buildings are on the National Register of Historic Places.

Continue southwest on US 30 to **York** *(Chamber of Commerce 717-848-4000 or 800-673-2429),* a country town that has bloomed into a city in recent decades. Several historic buildings date from its stint as the nation's capital from 1777 to 1778, when Congress fled Philadelphia after the British victory at Brandywine. One vestige of those early days is the **Horatio Gates House** *(157 W. Market St. 717-848-2951. Adm. fee),* where the hero of Saratoga lived. Next door, the **Golden Plough Tavern** *(157 W. Market St. 717-845-2951. Adm. fee)* is a frontier roadhouse furnished in period style. Across the street stands the **York County Colonial Court House** *(205 W. Market St. 717-846-1977. Closed Jan.-Feb.; adm. fee. Tickets at Gates house museum shop),* a 1976 reproduction of the courthouse where the Continental Congress convened. Another interesting, more modern, stop is the **Harley Davidson Motor Company & Museum** *(1425 Eden Rd. 717-848-1177 ext. 5900. Call for tours),* where the famous motorcycles are manufactured.

US 30 and Pa. 116 lead south to **Hanover,** home to pretzelmaker **Snyder's of Hanover** *(Pa. 116. 717-632-4477 or 800-233-7125),* a good place to stock up on snacks. Munch them lakeside at **Codorus State Park** *(SE of town on Pa. 216. 717-637-2816),* or drive on to **Hanover Shoe Farms** *(Pa. 194. 717-637-8931),* where some 1,800 horses and 4,000 acres make this home to record-setting pacers and trotters.

To the west is ❼ **Gettysburg**★★ *(Convention & Visitors Bureau 717-334-6274).* A crossroads town just north of the Mason-Dixon Line, it marks the improbable site of the bloodiest battle in the Civil War: 51,000 casualties fell here.

It started almost by accident. During the summer of 1863, Gen. Robert E. Lee's Confederate Army moved into Pennsylvania hoping to defeat the Union Forces on their own turf. Scavenging the area for supplies, some of Lee's troops headed toward Gettysburg on reconnaissance to count the numbers of the Union cavalry. Battle lines formed, and on July 1 more than 88,000 bluecoats faced off against 70,000 Rebels. The fighting raged for three days, until Lee retreated. Cemetery Ridge and Pickett's Charge soon became watchwords for national mourning and patriotism.

They still are. Each year about a million people flock here to witness the site of the conflict. But be forewarned, with 5,900 acres and 31 miles of marked roads, **Gettysburg National Military Park**★★ can be literally and emotionally daunting. Get an early start—town and battlefield are especially haunting as the morning mist begins to break. The park's main **Visitor Center** *(Pa. 134, S of town. 717-334-1124)* is the starting point for guided and self-guided tours, as well as home to a museum and the famous electric map *(fee)* that traces the three-day battle. The park itself nearly surrounds the town of Gettysburg, and is peppered with 1,600 monuments, many quite moving.

Gettysburg National Cemetery lies adjacent to the Visitor Center, where more than 3,000 Civil War dead are buried. The 60-foot, marble **Soldiers' National Monument** rises near where President Abraham Lincoln stood on November 19, 1863, to implore "that these dead

Gettysburg National Military Park

121

shall not have died in vain…," during his eloquent Gettysburg Address.

Serious Civil War buffs may want to visit the **Conflict Theater and Bookshop** *(213 Steinwehr/US 15. 717-334-8003. June-Aug., call for off-season hours; adm. fee),* featuring a four-program documentary on the battle and war. You can see where the Civil War President revised his famous speech at the **Lincoln Room Museum** *(12 Lincoln Sq. 717-334-8188. Closed Sat.-Sun. Dec.-Feb.; adm. fee).* Or peruse the memorabilia at **General Lee's Headquarters Museum** *(401 Buford Ave./US 30. 717-334-3141. Mid-March–Nov.; adm. fee).*

The **Eisenhower National Historic Site** ★ ★ *(Via shuttle bus from Gettysburg N.M.P. Visitor Center. 717-338-9114. Daily April-Oct., Wed.-Sun. Nov.-Dec. and Feb.-March; adm. fee)* encompasses the 231-acre farm and 1950s home of President Dwight D. Eisenhower and his wife, Mamie, with their furnishings and memorabilia.

Return to Harrisburg via US 15.

The Poconos

● **280 miles** ● **3 days** ● **Spring through fall**

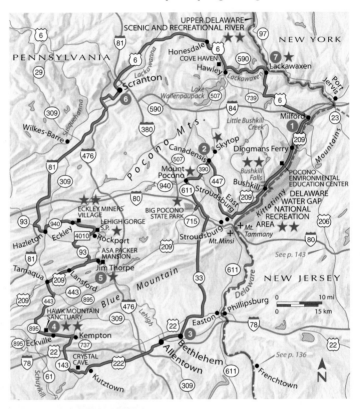

See p. 143

See p. 136

Grey Towers, Milford

Breathtaking mountain views, waterfalls framed by mountain laurel, rushing streams, and wooded valleys—the Pocono Mountains in northeastern Pennsylvania provide a wilderness escape about two hours from New York City and Philadelphia. With its resort hotels, golf courses, and ski resorts, the region is a prime vacation spot—and a fabled honeymoon destination.

From Milford, the drive will head south to explore the mountain falls, trails, and vistas of the Delaware Water Gap National Recreation Area. From here the route climbs west into 2,000-foot mountains, dotted with small villages, ski areas, and mountain resorts. You stop at the Moravian city of Bethlehem and then Hawk Mountain, where thousands of raptors fill the air during their fall migration. Farther ahead, several sites show how anthracite mining has been a way of life in the Poconos for centuries. In Scranton, the Lackawanna Coal Mine and Steamtown National Historic Site revive the glory days of mining and steam railroading. Finally, you drive among high country forests and lakes before descending through the gorges of the Upper Delaware Scenic and Recreational River.

The drive begins in ❶ **Milford** *(Chamber of Commerce 717-296-8700)*, where **Grey Towers** *(Old Owego Turnpike, off US 6. 717-296-9630. Renovation in progress)* recalls one of America's first leaders in environmental conservation. Future Gov. Gifford Pinchot moved into this 42-room, French château-style mansion overlooking the Delaware Valley with his family in 1886. Inside you'll find artwork, photographs, original furnishings, and family memorabilia. Sprawling over 102 acres of gardens and terraces, the estate now houses the Pinchot Institute for Conservation Studies. Pinchot helped start the U.S. Forest Service, which has done much to restore both local and national forests after devastating logging and mining in the early 1900s. **Sawkill Falls** are on the estate, and not far away, the **Upper Mill** *(150 Water St. 717-296-5141. Easter–Thanksgiving)* has a three-story waterwheel that has been churning grist on Sawkill Creek since the late 1800s.

Heading south on US 209, you enter the **Delaware Water Gap National Recreation Area** ★ ★ *(717-588-2451)*. Steep and wooded, the western valley slope presses you close to the Delaware River, where you pass islands and cornfields before reaching **Dingmans Ferry.** Here is the toll bridge to the New Jersey side of the wilderness, where backcountry roads provide opportunities for biking and cross-country skiing (see The Highlands drive, p. 143).

Among the 12 miles of trails at the **Pocono Environmental Education Center** *(US 209. 717-828-2319)*, farther south on US 209, is one that leads to an escarpment rich in marine fossils. The 2-mile **Scenic Gorge Trail** makes an easy walk through a stream-carved gorge covered with

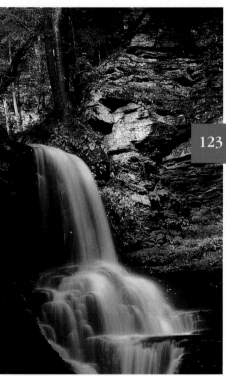

123

Bushkill Falls

hemlocks (the Pennsylvania state tree). The center is available to individuals, educational groups, and families.

As you near the village of Bushkill, follow the signs to **Bushkill Falls**★★ *(Bushkill Falls Rd., off US 209. 717-588-6682. April-Nov.; adm. fee)*, a series of eight cascades that fill a gorge. A short trail from the parking area leads to an overlook of Main Falls, the highest, which drops a hundred feet. Several trails explore the gorge and more falls via dramatic wooden bridges and catwalks suspended above Little Bushkill Creek and Pond Run Creek.

Just down US 209 lies the **Bushkill Visitor Center** *(717-588-7044)*, a good place to orient yourself to the Delaware Water Gap National Recreation Area, which covers 70,000 acres along both banks of a nearly 40-mile stretch of the Delaware River. The center has maps and brochures that highlight sightseeing, hiking, fishing, camping, canoeing, and rafting opportunities.

To avoid traffic south of the village of Bushkill, follow the signs that lead off US 209 toward Park Headquarters. This road keeps you in the parklands as it proceeds south about 10 miles. At this point, watch for the break in the

124

Watching for raptors at Hawk Mountain Sanctuary, near Eckville

Kittatinny Mountains and the twin peaks—**Mount Tammany** and **Mount Minsi**—that mark the actual water gap. Legend has it that this gap gave the Poconos their name; *Pocohanne* is a supposed corruption of a Native American word for "stream between two mountains," or "water gap."

Now make a loop into the mountains, following Pa.

447, Pa. 390, Pa. 940, Pa. 611, and Pa. 715 through Poconos resort country *(Pocono Mountain Vacation Bureau 800-762-6667).* Winding your way through villages such as **②** **Canadensis** (named after the local giant hemlock) and **Mount Pocono,** you pass ski areas and resorts. If you are looking for lodging, you have a choice ranging from accommodations with champagne glass whirlpools to traditional mountain resorts such as **Skytop**★ *(Pa. 390. 717-595-7401 or 800-345-7759),* whose immense stone lodge, lake, and 5,500 acres spread over wild mountain peaks. For great mountain vistas, don't bypass **Big Pocono State Park**★ *(Off Pa. 715. 717-894-8336. Mid-April–mid-Dec.),* 1,306 rugged acres atop 2,131-foot Camelback Mountain. A 1.4-mile paved scenic drive loops the mountain summit, offering outstanding views that extend all the way to the Delaware Water Gap and the Catskills.

Go south on Pa. 33 and US 22 to **③** **Bethlehem** *(Visitor Center 610-868-1513 or 800-360-8687).* Now part of the urban-suburban quilt, Bethlehem is still worth a stop to see where Moravian missionaries from Central Europe penetrated the wilderness to set up their commune and spread the gospel to the Native Americans. They also built a flourishing industrial community by Monocacy Creek, which has been restored as the **Colonial Moravian Industrial Quarter** *(459 Old York Rd. 610-691-0603. Mon.-Fri.; adm. fee),* and includes a tannery, gristmill, and waterworks. In the center of town, the **Moravian Museum of Bethlehem**★ *(66 W. Church St. 610-867-0173. Tues.-Sat.; adm. fee)* stands among a compound of stone buildings dating from 1741. At the museum you see how the congregation lived together in "choirs" according to age and gender. The music room highlights their love of music, which persists today with **Bethlehem's Bach Festival** in May and **Musikfest** in August. During the December **Yuletide Festival,** the town glitters with hundreds of lighted trees and features a live Christmas pageant.

Farther west, stop at one of Pennsylvania's most popular caverns, **Crystal Cave** *(Pa. 143. 610-683-6765. March-Nov.; adm. fee),* to cool off among crystalline formations. A guided tour takes you past Prairie Dogs, Bridal Veil, and other limestone sculptures.

Now head northwest on Pa. 143 and Pa. 737 through rolling farms and woodlands. Soon you're climbing to the summit of Hawk Mountain, site of **④** **Hawk Mountain Sanctuary**★★ *(Off Pa. 737 at 1700 Hawk Mountain Rd. 610-756-6961. Adm. fee).* Designated a National Natural Landmark, this 2,380-acre preserve is a famous spot to observe the fall

---

Cupid Country

Before heading overseas during World War II, GIs liked to take their families and girlfriends to the Poconos for some R&R. After the war, the Poconos conjured sentimental memories for these folks, who returned for honeymoons and vacations. Thus began the Poconos' rivalry with Niagara Falls as "Honeymoon Capital of the World." In the early 1960s the first heart-shaped tub appeared at a honeymoon resort called Cove Haven, and *Life* magazine's photo feature on the phenomenon seized the imagination of lovers and developers. The Poconos now boast 13 ski areas, 35 golf courses, at least 170 tennis courts, more than a dozen canoe and raft outfitters, five riding stables, over 100 factory outlets, and nine luxury couples resorts.

Eckley Miners' Village, near Hazleton

migration of birds of prey. Between mid-August and mid-December an average of 20,000 hawks, falcons, and eagles pass through here. Working scientists, naturalists, a Visitor Center, and lookout trails make this sanctuary a popular place year-round; come early on weekends or holidays to assure a parking space.

The drive weaves north on Pa. 895, Pa. 443, and Pa. 309 into the 19th-century domain of anthracite mining. Anthracite was discovered in northeastern Pennsylvania after the Revolution. This clean-burning soft coal soon became desired nationwide; by the mid-1800s the region bustled with mines and factories. Most of the mines are closed now, and you will see that reclamation projects and nature have begun healing the land. But you pass by old coal company patch (privately owned) towns, which sprang up around individual mining stakes; many are still rimmed with "culm banks," mountains of slate dug from deep within the mountains and discarded.

The coal industry's mistreatment of laborers drove a group of Irish immigrant miners to form a chapter of the Molly Maguires, a secret organization that began in Ireland. They practiced violence against the coal companies from 1860 to 1875. In the town of **Tamaqua,** a historical plaque at Broad and Lehigh Streets marks the spot where three Mollies ambushed a policeman.

The drive proceeds northeast on US 209 to **Lansford,** where the **No. 9 Mine 'Wash Shanty' Anthracite Coal Mining Museum** *(9 Dock St. 717-645-7074. Wed.-Sun.; adm. fee)* explores the area's coal-mining heritage.

You will want to linger in the Victorian town of
5 **Jim Thorpe**★. Renamed in the 1950s for the great Olympic athlete, the former towns of Mauch Chunk and East Mauch Chunk sit in a steep hollow on the Lehigh River. The communities prospered in the 19th century as commercial and shipping centers for surrounding coal mines. As tourists discovered the area's mountains and streams in the late 1800s, the towns became known as the Switzerland of America.

Start your visit at the **Welcome Center** *(Market Sq., off*

US 209. 717-325-3673 or 888-546-8467), located in the old railroad station. Pick up a walking tour map of the historic district—mansion after mansion along the town's main street, dubbed Millionaires Row. Here, too, you can buy tickets for a scenic train ride through neighboring mountains aboard **Rail Tours, Inc.** *(717-325-4606 or 717-325-3673. May-Oct. weekends; fare).*

For a good grasp of the town's history, visit the **Mauch Chunk Museum & Cultural Center** *(41 W. Broadway. 717-325-9190. Mid-April–May Sat.-Sun., June-Oct. Thurs.-Sun.; adm. fee),* which has 19th-century travel souvenirs and mining artifacts. Seven Mollies were hung for alleged murders at the **Old Jail Museum** *(128 W. Broadway. 717-325-5259. Mid-May–Oct. Thurs.-Tues.; adm. fee),* in operation from 1871 to 1995. One of the condemned proclaimed that his hand print would remain on the wall as a sign of his innocence, and the print remains to this day.

The 1860 Italianate **Asa Packer Mansion** *(Packer Hill, off Pa. 209. 717-325-3229. Weekends April-May and Nov., daily June-Oct.; adm. fee)* belonged to a tycoon whose life changed from rags to riches with the coal boom.

Leaving town, backtrack on US 209 and go north on Pa. 93 and County Rd. 4010 to **Lehigh Gorge State Park ★** *(Off County Rd. 4010, Rockport. 717-427-5000).* Mountain bikers and hikers enjoy a converted railroad bed along Lehigh Gorge, while Class III rapids challenge white-water enthusiasts; contact the park for outfitting information.

Next head west on Pa. 940 to **Eckley Miners' Village ★★** *(Off Pa. 940. 717-636-2070. Adm. fee).* Settled in 1854, Eckley was a coal company patch town until 1971. Retired miners and their survivors still keep house in some of the 50-plus weathered buildings, comprising a living history museum of the first order. Visitor Center exhibits glimpse into a worker's home life; you can

Steamtown National Historic Site, Scranton

also tour a doctor's office and an 1890 two-family home.

Head north on I-81 to **⑥ Scranton,** where you complete your visit to the world of anthracite mining. Stop at the **Anthracite Heritage Museum** *(Off Keyser Ave. in*

127

McDade Park. 717-963-4804. Adm. fee) to learn about the immigrants who moved to northeastern Pennsylvania to find work in the mines. At the neighboring **Lackawanna Coal Mine**★ *(717-963-6463 or 800-238-7245. April-Nov.; adm. fee)*, ride a railcar 300 feet below the earth's surface to experience a miner's work firsthand. In the center of town, the **Steamtown National Historic Site**★★ *(Cliff St. and Lackawanna Ave. 717-340-5200. Adm. fee)* serves as a reminder of the days when America's transportation system depended on coal. Occupying the former railroad yard of the Delaware Lackawanna & Western Railroad, Steamtown showcases 27 steam locomotives—including the Union Pacific's "Big Boy," one of the largest steam locomotives ever built. The Technology Museum contains a model of the rail yard in its 1930s heyday, and the History Museum focuses on the development of railroading in the U.S. You can also take a ride behind a live steamer. Just up the street stand the mid-1800s **Scranton Iron Furnaces** *(Cedar Ave. 717-963-4804)*, which burned anthracite into iron ore and fueled the city's boom as an industrial center.

Head out of town on US 6 to **Honesdale,** where America's first commercial steam locomotive ran in 1829. **Stourbridge Rail Excursions** *(303 Commercial St. 717-253-1960 or 800-433-9008. Selected weekends June-Dec.; fare)* offers rides on vintage cars. At the junction with Pa. 590 lies the Victorian village of **Hawley** *(Information center 717-226-3191)*, filled with antique shops and B&Bs. The town is also the hub of a recreation area that includes **Lake Wallenpaupack,** one of the state's largest lakes, and the Upper Delaware River.

Follow Pa. 590 out of Hawley for about 3 miles, and bear right on an unmarked road that winds along the pretty Lackawaxen River. In ❼ **Lackawaxen**★ the river converges with the **Upper Delaware Scenic and Recreational River**★★ *(717-685-4871)*, a 73.4-mile stretch along the New York–Pennsylvania border.

Pick up overflowing deli sandwiches at Beckley's Lackawaxen General Store *(1 Scenic Dr. 717-685-1350)* and continue down the road to the **Zane Grey House**★ *(Scenic Dr. 717-685-4871. June-Aug. daily, spring and fall weekends)*, which offers an exceptional picnic area. The writer retreated to this mansion between 1905 and 1918, and it now holds memorabilia from his adventurous life. Flossy grass and shade trees abound along the Delaware River. Sit back and watch bald eagles soar, and measure time by the canoeists gliding south on the current between endless hills of green. Then return to Milford via Pa. 590 and US 6.

At the Zane Grey House, Lackawaxen

Philadelphia Freedom Trail ★★

● **140 miles** ● **2 to 3 days** ● **Year-round**

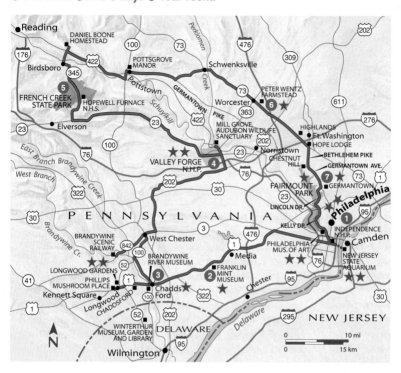

Enthusiasm for liberty is inherent in Philadelphia's past and present, and this trip provides a fascinating look at the city's pivotal place in American history. Beginning with the Liberty Bell, Independence Hall, and Betsy Ross's home in downtown Philadelphia, the trail leads west to the Franklin Mint Museum and the Brandywine Valley, with its Revolutionary War battlefield, famous châteaus, and art museum. Passing through well-groomed West Chester, the route heads north to Valley Forge, then east, traveling amid rural villages rife with historic houses and antique shops. You return to Philadelphia through its historic neighborhoods, ending at Fairmount Park.

Visitors to ❶ **Philadelphia**★★ *(Visitor Center 215-636-1666)* should begin their tour at the city's new waterfront park, **Penn's Landing**★★ *(Market and Lombard Sts. 215-629-3200)*, with two big parking lots just off I-95. Among the historic vessels docked here are the USS *Becuna* and the USS *Olympia*, a cruiser important in securing a decisive naval

Liberty Bell

Logan Circle fountain and Philadelphia Museum of Art

victory during the Spanish and American War. The **Independence Seaport Museum** *(211 S. Columbus Blvd. at Walnut St. 215-925-5439. Adm. fee)* further explores the nation's maritime history. Stroll and eat a braided pretzel from a vendor's cart or take a narrated lunch or dinner cruise aboard the ***Spirit of Philadelphia*** *(Columbus Blvd. 215-923-1419),* leaving from the landing. Or hop the ferry across the Delaware to see a huge fish tank with two dozen sharks and a shipwreck at the **New Jersey State Aquarium**★★ *(1 Riverside Dr., Camden, N.J. 609-365-3300. Adm. fee).*

Back in Philadelphia, the L-shaped **Independence National Historical Park** *(215-597-8974 for information on all park sites)* contains more than 20 buildings that illuminate the founding and early history of the United States. Start at the **Visitor Center** *(Third and Chestnut Sts.),* just blocks west of Penn's Landing. View the worthwhile film, *Independence;* pick up a walking tour map; and orient yourself to the park, which centers around **Independence Hall**★★ *(Chestnut St. bet. 5th and 6th Sts. By tour only; renovations underway, phone Visitor Center for schedule).* Built between 1732 and 1756 as the Pennsylvania State House, Independence Hall may be the most significant building in American history, where the Declaration of Independence was signed and the U.S. Constitution drafted. Inside, the Assembly Room has been restored much as it was between 1775 and 1787, including the ink stand where signers penned their names on the revolutionary documents.

Next door, **Congress Hall**★ was home to the U.S. Senate and House of Representatives between 1790 and 1800, when Philadelphia was the nation's capital. It was here that Congress ratified the Bill of Rights (1791) and signed the Jay Treaty (1794). This is also where Washington was sworn in for his second term, and where he later delivered his Farewell Address.

The **Liberty Bell Pavilion**★★ stands across the street from Independence Hall. The bell that rang from the State House to gather the citizens of Philadelphia for a public reading of the Declaration of Independence, on July 8, 1776, was moved to this glass structure for America's bicentennial, where it can be viewed at any time of day. Rangers and audiotapes in 16 languages relate the bell's story.

A host of other important historic sites fill the neighborhood. The Greek Revival **Second Bank of the**

Don't Blame Congress

A glance at Philadelphia's role in American history yields an impressive résumé: The first Continental Congress met here in 1774, the second Continental Congress signed the Declaration of Independence here in 1776, and the Constitutional Convention approved the new Constitution here in 1787. Except during the British occupation in 1777, Philadelphia remained the seat of the colonial congress. George Washington lived in town during both his terms of office as president. Given all this, why is Philadelphia not the U.S. capital? The answer may lie in the proximity of the District of Columbia to Washington's beloved Virginia. Responsible for picking the capital site, the Virginia farmer chose with his heart—and the capital was moved to Washington, D.C.

United States *(Chestnut St. bet. 4th and 5th Sts.)* houses the national historical park's portrait gallery. Many of the 185 paintings of the nation's early leaders are by Charles Willson Peale, who founded the nation's first museum in 1802, in Independence Hall. **Franklin Court**★ *(Market St. bet. 3rd and 4th Sts.)* is a compound of five Franklin-era buildings where you view a film about Franklin's life and see a newspaper office, post office, and print shop from libertarian days. But the most striking structure here is one you can see through—architect Robert Venturi's delineation in steel framework of the only house Benjamin Franklin ever owned. Cutaways show the original foundations, and an underground museum presents interesting exhibits on Franklin's life and ideas.

Nearby, but not part of the park, the **Betsy Ross House**★ *(239 Arch St. 215-627-5343. Closed Mon.; donation)* contains the famed flagmaker's original spectacles, and is furnished according to the period. Down the street, the **United States Mint** *(5th and Arch Sts. 215-597-7350. July-Aug. daily, May-June Mon.-Sat., Sept.-April Mon.-Fri.)* offers self-guided tours. Mixed among these historic sites stand a collection of significant museums, including the **Afro-American Historical and Cultural Museum** *(701 Arch St. 215-574-0380. Closed Mon.; adm. fee),* the **National Museum of American Jewish History** *(55 N. 5th St., on Independence Mall E. 215-923-3811. Closed Sat.; adm. fee),* and the **Curtis Center Museum of Norman Rockwell Art** *(6th and Sansom Sts. 215-922-4345. Adm. fee).*

Brandywine River Museum interior, Chadds Ford

Before leaving downtown, walk among the federal period town houses of **Society Hill**★ *(Bounded by Walnut, Front, Lombard, and 6th Sts.),* take in the scents of flowers and fresh produce at the **Reading Terminal Market**★ *(51 N. 12th St. at Arch St. 215-922-2317. Closed Sun.),* or wander through the city's exceptional art museums. A short drive west, the **Rodin Museum** *(Benjamin Franklin Pkwy. and 22nd St. 215-763-8100. Closed Mon.; donation)* has the largest collection of the sculptor's work outside of Paris. It is an adjunct museum to what most authorities rank as one of the great art collections of the world, the **Philadelphia Museum of Art**★★ *(Benjamin Franklin Pkwy. and 26th St. 215-763-8100. Closed Mon.; adm. fee except Sun. a.m.).* The spectacular holdings of the latter include paintings, sculpture, prints, and drawings from Europe, Asia, and the U.S., spanning more than 2,000 years.

While in the area, check out the **Upstages** *(Liberty Place, 2nd Floor. 215-893-1145)* kiosk at 16th and Chestnut Streets for half-price, same-day theater tickets.

A short drive on US 1 south leads to Media and the ❷ **Franklin Mint Museum**★ *(US 1. 610-459-6168).* Filled with beautiful collectibles, the exhibits include everything from porcelain dolls and jewelry to die-cast models of motor vehicles, historic weapon reproductions, and art by Andrew Wyeth and Norman Rockwell.

Longwood Gardens in bloom

Leaving the museum, continue south on US 1, entering the château country of the **Brandywine Valley**★★. Amid these rolling pastures, woods, and streams lie the legendary mansions of the du Pont family. In ❸ **Chadds Ford**★, the 50-acre **Brandywine Battlefield State Park** *(US 1. 610-459-3342. Closed Mon.)* includes the farmhouses that served as headquarters for George Washington and the Marquis de Lafayette during the battle of September 11, 1777. Perhaps the Continental Army's greatest defeat, it left the road to Philadelphia open to the redcoats. Every year in mid-September there are reenactments of the battle, which is described in exhibits at the Visitor Center.

Nearby, the **Brandywine River Museum** *(US 1. 610-388-2700. Adm. fee)* is famous for its collection of works by three generations of the Wyeth family. Housed in what was originally a Civil War-era gristmill, the museum also features other American artists, such as Howard Pyle and Maxfield Parrish. Farther down on US 1 south, the **Chaddsford Winery** *(610-388-6221. Closed Mon.; tasting fee)* offers a great place to relax. Operating from a renovated 18th-century barn, this boutique winery supplies tables for picnics and some weekend concerts.

To really relax, take as much time as you can for a wander through **Longwood Gardens**★★ *(US 1, Kennett Square. 610-388-1000. Adm. fee)*. This is America's ultimate garden, with 1,050 outdoor acres, 20 indoor gardens, and dramatic, illuminated fountains. There are 11,000 different kinds of plants, roses, and orchids in bloom year-round, an Idea Garden for home gardeners, an indoor Children's Garden with a maze, the historic Pierre du Pont House, and a mighty pipe organ. Each season brings new colors, while seasonal festivals and concerts add to the spectacle.

You can learn about another Brandywine specialty—mushrooms—at the **Phillips Mushroom Place** *(909 E. Baltimore Pike/US 1. 610-388-6082. Adm. fee)*. Here a film, models, and photos help explore local fungus farming lore.

Backtrack to Pa. 100 and wind north to **West Chester** *(Chamber of Commerce 610-696-4046)*, a polished town of 18,500 that includes many pristine Victorian and Greek Revival houses as well as a downtown district for upscale shoppers. For two of the best ways to see the Brandywine Valley, travel just a few miles west of town to the **Northbrook Canoe Co.** *(Northbrook Rd., off Pa. 842. 610-793-2279)*. They offer canoe and tube rentals for floating down the river, as well as a more luxurious passage aboard the **Brandywine Scenic Railway** *(610-793-4433. Call for schedule; fare)*. A picnic basket will enhance the hour-long ride.

The drive up US 202, US 422, and Valley Forge Road (Pa. 23) brings you to the log shelters of the Continental Army and a new understanding of the phrase "Philadelphia freedom." ❹ **Valley Forge National Historical Park**★★ *(Pa. 23. 610-783-1077)* encompasses 3,500 acres of fields and meadows. Start your tour at the **Visitor Center** *(Pa. 23 and N. Gulph Rd.)*. Here you can join a bus tour or pick up a tape for a self-guided automobile tour of the encampment where Washington and his Continentals came to lick their wounds after their loss at Brandywine and stalemate at Germantown. During the the six-month encampment in the bitter winter of 1777-78, about 2,000 soldiers died from the poor conditions here, but the army

---

Not Your Average Collector

One of the heirs to the du Pont fortune, Henry Francis du Pont began collecting early American decorative arts in the 1920s. His collection soon outgrew his ancestral manor, and he decided to expand the building to house 175 period rooms. The result, across the border in Delaware, is **Winterthur Museum, Garden and Library**★★ *(Del. 52, 6 miles N of Wilmington. 302-888-4600 or 800-448-3883. Adm. fee)*, the Brandywine Valley's most famous attraction. The country estate, opened to the public in 1951, displays du Pont's holdings of American furniture, textiles, silver, needlework, porcelain, Oriental rugs, and paintings—more than 89,000 objects.

133

Valley Forge cannon

Daniel Boone Homestead, Birdsboro

hung on, reorganized into an efficient fighting force, and kept the British immobilized in Philadelphia. More than 3,000 artifacts from Revolutionary War days are on view at the **Valley Forge Historical Society Museum** *(610-783-0535. Adm. fee)*, located inside the park's Washington Memorial Chapel.

Drive north on US 422 and Pawlings Road to where the 175-acre **Mill Grove, Audubon Wildlife Sanctuary** *(Pawlings and Audubon Rds. 610-666-5593. Closed Mon.)* lies just north of Valley Forge on Perkiomen Creek. Young John James Audubon came here in 1804 from France to manage the estate for his father. Here he courted and married his wife and developed his passion for American birds and wildlife. The house contains a collection of the artist's work and memorabilia, and miles of trails traverse the grounds, where more than 175 species of birds and some 400 species of flowering plants have been identified.

Proceed west on Pa. 23 through rolling fields and past 18th-century stone houses that preside over family farms. The terrain grows more rugged as you turn north on Pa. 345 into the forested lands of ❺ **French Creek State Park** *(Park Rd., Elverson. 610-582-9680)*. With 7,339 acres, 30 miles of marked trails, two lakes, and camping areas, the park makes a great escape for nature lovers. A nearby attraction is **Hopewell Furnace National Historic Site** *(Pa. 345, 5 miles S of Birdsboro. 610-582-8773. Adm. fee)*, a restored 18th- and 19th-century ironmaking village that cast everything from hollowware to Revolutionary War shot and cannons. You can see an audiovisual program at the Visitor Center, watch molding and casting demonstrations inside the restored buildings, and tour the houses and shops.

A number of historic houses lie along the route back toward Philadelphia. North of Birdsboro, the **Daniel Boone Homestead** *(400 Daniel Boone Rd. 610-582-4900. Closed Mon.; adm. fee)* preserves the 579-acre farm where the famous frontiersman was born in 1734. It includes a Visitor Center, lake, picnic areas, and several 18th-century buildings that interpret the life of the Quaker Boone family and their contemporaries.

Next follow US 422 east and Pa. 100 north to Pottstown, where a very different style of colonial life existed at the elegant **Pottsgrove Manor** *(Pa. 100 and W. King St. 610-326-4014. Closed Mon.),* built in 1752 by John Potts, a colonial ironmaster and founder of Pottstown. Inside, the Georgian interior provides a backdrop for an extensive collection of two centuries of decorative arts. In the nearby town of Schwenksville, **Pennypacker Mills** *(Pa. 73 at Haldeman Rd. 610-287-9349. Closed Mon.)* is a colonial revival mansion with family furnishings that reflect the Victorian age.

Near the Philadelphia city line stand three houses that played roles in the quest for American independence. The **❻ Peter Wentz Farmstead★** *(Off Pa. 73 and Pa. 363. 610-584-5104. Closed Mon.)* in Worcester is where Washington planned the Battle of Germantown in the fall of 1777; at the Georgian **Highlands** *(7001 Sheaf Ln. 215-641-2687. Mon.-Fri.; adm. fee)* in Fort Washington, Speaker of the House Anthony Morris entertained Jefferson, Madison, and Monroe; and, just south of Fort Washington, **Hope Lodge** *(553 Bethlehem Pike. 215-646-1595. Closed Mon.; adm. fee)* is an early Georgian mansion that served as Washington's surgeon general's headquarters in 1777.

135

Now take Bethlehem Pike south to Germantown Avenue, through the once fashionable enclave of **❼ Germantown★**—site of the 1777 Battle of Germantown. For a clearer picture of the battle, visit **Cliveden★** *(640 Germantown Ave. 215-848-1777. April-Dec. Thurs.-Sun.; adm. fee).* Home of colonial Chief Justice Benjamin Chew, the stone mansion stopped bullets during the battle. Today, the restored house serves as the Historic Germantown headquarters, which provides information on other historic sites in Germantown.

Reenter central Philadelphia by taking Lincoln Drive through a twisting, wooded ravine to Kelly Drive and **Fairmount Park★** *(215-685-0000).* With 8,579 acres, this park nestled on the Schuyl-

Horse sculpture in Fairmount Park

kill River was home to the 1876 Centennial Exposition and includes colonial houses, outdoor music venues, waterworks, rock gardens, a horticultural hall, and a zoo. Miles of woods and riverside trails lead past the rowing clubs on Boat House Row.

● **275 miles** ● **3 to 4 days** ● **Spring through autumn**

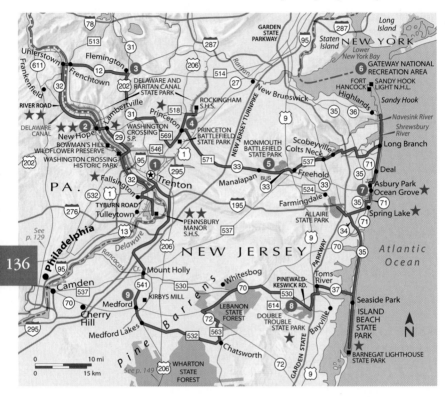

This drive unveils central New Jersey's subtle beauty, as well as its historical significance and cultural traditions. Beginning in the state capital of Trenton, you crisscross over the Delaware River in and out of Pennsylvania, exploring William Penn's manor, the site of Gen. George Washington's historic crossing of the Delaware River, and the artist colony of New Hope. The route then circles east through woods and farms, pausing at Princeton and Monmouth Battlefield. Taking off among horse farms and estates, you reach the Jersey shore, where Sandy Hook and its beach await. The drive bears south through a variety of beach resorts, including Deal and Ocean Grove, to the coastal wilderness of Island Beach State Park. The return to Trenton tunnels through the Pine Barrens, stopping at a ghost town and the cranberry center of Chatsworth.

Situated at the head of navigation on the Delaware River, ❶ **Trenton** *(Visitor Center 609-777-1770)* earned a reputation early on as a smoky, industrial city. While remaining more devoted to brawn than beauty, it holds

some appeal for travelers. The core
of the golden-domed **New Jersey State House**
*(W. State St. 609-633-2709. Tours Mon.-Sat. July-Aug., Tues.-Wed.
and Fri.-Sat. June and Sept.)* dates from 1792, and ongoing
restoration has brought about commissioned artworks,
refurbished legislative wings, and re-created period rooms.
The adjoining **Stacy Park,** a green haven for strolling and
lounging, unites the Capitol Complex. Don't miss the
nearby four-story **New Jersey State Museum** *(205 W. State
St. 609-292-6464. Closed Mon.),* which began in the mid-1800s
with a small collection of mineral samples. Its vast collection covers archaeology, fine arts, cultural history, and natural science. A strong collection of Native American
artifacts, amber, two mastodon skeletons, and a planetarium are among highlights.

On the other side of the State House stands the **Old
Barracks Museum★** *(Barrack St. 609-396-1776. Adm. fee),*
built during the French and Indian War and variously
occupied by British, Hessian, and American troops during
the Revolutionary War. The barracks were a focal point of
combat after Gen. George Washington crossed the

137

Delaware River near General Washington's crossing

Delaware in 1776 and attacked Trenton. His defeat of
Hessian soldiers here reinvigorated the war-tattered American troops, leading to a series of stunning victories.
Today, role-playing interpreters give first-person accounts
of life during the Revolution.

If you've got an appetite, drive a few blocks south to
Historic Chambersburg *(S of Hamilton Ave., W of S. Clinton*

Ave.), New Jersey's Little Italy, where you can pick from a dozen popular restaurants. Nearby, the circa 1719 Georgian colonial **Trent House** *(15 Market St. 609-989-3027. Adm. fee)* belonged to William Trent, the city's founding father. Period furnishings portray the life of a wealthy merchant.

Now follow US 1 across the Delaware River into Pennsylvania, picking up US 13 south to Tyburn Road east. Signs lead to **Pennsbury Manor State Historic Site**★★ *(Just E of Tulleytown. 215-946-0400. Closed Mon.; adm. fee),* William Penn's 43-acre estate on the Delaware. While history associates Penn with the founding of the Quaker colony that became Pennsylvania, Penn was also active in administering the affairs of the New Jersey colony. Costumed interpreters lead visitors through the manor house, bake-and-brew house, formal garden, and farm. A waterfront park has attractive picnic sites.

A few miles north of Pennsbury awaits historic **Fallsington**★ *(Off Tyburn Rd. 215-295-6567. Tours May-Oct.; adm. fee).* This is not a commercial re-created village, but a living Quaker settlement whose stone meetinghouse, tavern, and houses date back to the 1600s. With its tall shade trees, green spaces, and enduring architecture, Fallsington is as close as you can come to Brigadoon in America.

Retrace your steps to US 1 and head north on Pa. 32 along the river. Soon you come to **Washington Crossing Historic Park** *(215-493-4076. Buildings closed Mon.; fee for buildings),* where on Christmas night in 1776, George Washington and 2,400 Continentals secretly crossed the ice-clogged Delaware River to attack Trenton. You can visit several historic buildings, including the **McConkey Ferry Inn,** where Washington is believed to have dined before the crossing. The Visitor Center has a film, and there are plenty of picnic sites along the riverbank. In the park's northern section, **Bowman's Hill Wildflower**

Covered bridge, Bucks County

Preserve *(5 miles N on Pa. 32. 215-862-2924),* you'll find 100 woodsy acres for hiking and walking.

Follow Washington—by bridge (Pa. 532/N.J. 546)— and cross the Delaware to New Jersey. At what's now

Washington Crossing State Park *(N.J. 546. 609-737-9303. Wed.-Sun.; parking fee weekends Mem. Day–Labor Day)*, the Continental Army set out on their march to Trenton; in the park the first mile of their route is preserved as **Continental Lane,** marked with commemorative plaques. The **Visitor Center/Museum** interprets the historic events that began here and displays more than 900 artifacts from the Revolutionary War period. One of the historic houses open for tours is the 1740 **Johnson Ferry House** *(Wed.-Sun.)*, refurbished as an inn. Boasting 841 acres of open fields and forest, the park also offers hiking, biking, fishing, and picnicking; the **Open Air Theater** *(609-737-1826. Mid-June–mid-Aug.)* presents summer concerts and plays.

Firestone Library, Princeton University

Driving north along the Delaware River on N.J. 29, you notice a feeder canal paralleling the road. This band of water and its towpath are one branch of the **Delaware & Raritan Canal** *(732-873-3050)*, completed in 1834 to promote commerce between Philadelphia and New York City. It's now a state park with two sections, both highly popular among hikers, canoeists, kayakers, and fishermen.

139

You will sense a change of atmosphere when you reach **Lambertville**★ *(Chamber of Commerce 609-397-0055)*. Founded in the 1700s, this former water-powered industrial town has shed its muscles in favor of gentrification. It's fun to stroll the streets, where 18th- and 19th-century buildings host a collection of art galleries, antique dealers, specialty shops, cafés, and B&Bs.

You could spend a week exploring ❷ **New Hope**★★ *(Chamber of Commerce 215-862-5880)*, across the river in Pennsylvania. The many art galleries, shops, bistros, chic restaurants, crafts people, night cabarets, and inns have transformed the 19th-century village into an eclectic artist colony and major weekend destination for New Yorkers. You can take hot-air balloon rides *(Color the Sky, Doylestown. 215-340-9966. Fee)*, float down the **Delaware Canal** in a mule-drawn barge *(New Hope Barge Co., S. Main St. 215-862-2842. April–mid-Nov.; fee)*, or hop a steam-powered dinner train aboard the **New Hope & Ivyland Railroad** *(W. Bridge and Stockton Sts. 215-862-2332. Mid-May–Oct. daily, call for off-season schedule; fare)*. By night catch a play at the **Bucks County Playhouse** *(70 S. Main St. 215-862-2041. May-Dec.)*.

Leading north for 25 miles along the Delaware, **River Road**★★ *(Pa. 32)* is one of the mid-Atlantic's prettiest drives. The route explores lovely Bucks County, twisting between wooded valley slopes and farms dotted with 18th-century stone houses. Take any of the side roads up the hollows to encounter one of the area's famous covered bridges. A number of farms and historic houses have become cozy B&Bs, including **Frankenfield Farm** (93 Frankenfield Rd., Frankenfield. 610-847-2771). For information on other B&Bs in Bucks County, call 800-982-1235.

At Uhlerstown the route crosses back into New Jersey to **Frenchtown,** a budding Lambertville, before climbing through farm country to ❸ **Flemington,** site of the 1935 Lindbergh kidnapping trial. Here, weekend steam train rides are offered aboard the **Black River & Western Railroad** (N.J. 12 and Stangle Rd. 908-782-9600. Easter–mid-Dec.; fare).

Next head south through rolling woodland to ❹ **Princeton**★ (Chamber of Commerce 609-520-1776). This bustling university town has its share of history—a decisive Revolutionary War battle took place here in 1777, and in 1783 it hosted the Continental Congress (making the small town the U.S. capital for several months). A good first stop is **Bainbridge House** (158 Nassau St. 609-921-6748. Closed Mon.), the restored 1766 birthplace of William Bainbridge—commander of the USS Constitution during the War of 1812. It now houses a museum and serves as headquarters for the Historical Society of Princeton, staffed by friendly people.

Having been driven from Philadelphia by civil unrest, the Continental Congress met in **Nassau Hall** at **Princeton University** (Off Nassau St. 609-258-3603), where they received General Washington. The 1756 building—which also served as British headquarters during the Revolutionary War—now houses an administrative office. You can visit the hall as part of a free tour offered by the Orange Key Guide Service (McLean House. 609-258-3603).

While on campus, don't miss the **Princeton Art Museum** (McCormick Hall. 609-258-3787. Closed Mon.), with its collection of Chinese bronzes, Greek and Roman antiquities, tomb figures, and Renaissance paintings.

Shortly after their victory at Trenton, Washington's forces won another battle at Princeton, marking an important turning point in the Revolutionary War. **Princeton Battlefield State Park** (500 Mercer Rd. 609-921-0074. Tours Wed.-Sun.) commemorates this event. On the grounds, the **Thomas Clarke House** is a working farm and site of the field hospital where Gen. Hugh Mercer died from wounds after the battle. The **Rockingham State Historic Site** (5 miles N of town at 108 County Rd. 518. 609-921-8835. Wed.-Sun.) preserves a gentleman farmer's house, which Washington used as a headquarters in 1783. While the Continental Congress met in Princeton, Wash-

Jersey Devil

Since colonial days the Jersey Devil has haunted the Pine Barrens. A winged beast with tail and claws, it has been blamed for the deaths of livestock and humans that venture too far down the area's jumble of sandy trails. While the Jersey Devil is a myth, the Pine Barrens are notorious for harboring lawless men. Joe Milliner—the "Robin Hood" of the pines—hid out here in the late 1700s; after coming out of the forest for a local tavern dance, he was caught and hung. If you want to tempt the devil, consider a moonlit nature walk from the general store in Whitesbog (off N.J. 530. 609-893-4646. Fee).

ington wrote his "Farewell Orders to the Armies" here.

Head west out of Princeton toward the shore. Passing through farmland, the drive reaches ❺ **Monmouth Battlefield State Park** *(Bus. N.J. 33. 908-462-9616),* where George Washington defeated Sir Henry Clinton in June 1778. It was during this combat that legendary Molly Pitcher distinguished herself by carrying water to the Continentals and fighting in her husband's place. The battlefield has a Visitor Center, hiking trails, picnic area, and nature center.

When Gen. Henry Clinton's redcoats fled Monmouth, they retreated to Sandy Hook. Follow their route along County Rd. 537 through horse farms. North on N.J. 36 you reach the redcoats' departure point for New York, **Sandy Hook.** Now part of the ❻ **Gateway National Recreation Area** *(908-872-0115. June-Aug.; summer parking fee),* this 6-mile, barrier beach peninsula forms the lower lip of New York Harbor—providing quite a contrast between its coastal wilderness and Manhattan's skyscrapers just up the way. If you want to venture into Manhattan, Express Navigation *(732-872-2628 or 800-BOAT RIDE. Fare)* runs high-speed ferries from docks near the shops and restaurants of Highlands, across the Shrewsbury River.

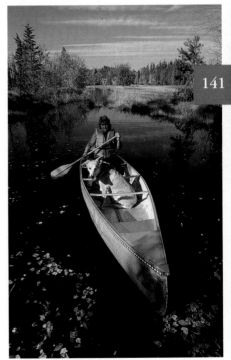

141

The longtime site of Fort Hancock—a keystone in the defense of New York— Gateway has become an oasis for bathers, clammers, surf anglers, and 300 species of birds. The old fort, Sandy Hook Light, the Spermaceti Cove Visitor Center, and the Sandy Hook Museum provide a nice break.

Leaving Sandy Hook, follow the shoreline south, passing through resort towns whose characters change faster than the traffic lights along the way. **Deal** has the look of Palm Beach. Once a celebrated resort, **Asbury Park** is a shadow of its former self; Bruce Springsteen and Jon

Paddling through the Pine Barrens

Bon Jovi got their starts here at the **Stone Pony** bar *(913 Ocean Ave. 908-775-5700).*

To step back into the 1880s and its Christian camp meetings, spend some time walking around ❼ **Ocean Grove★** *(Chamber of Commerce 908-774-1391).* The village has only a half mile of beach, but the hundreds of Victorian cottages and elaborate tent-houses mark a National Historic Landmark. Summer concerts in the 6,500-seat

Great Auditorium *(908-775-0035)* have featured the likes of Mel Torme, Tony Bennett, and the Kingston Trio.

On a much grander scale, **Spring Lake** ★ *(Chamber of Commerce 908-449-0577)* stands as a living monument to the Victorian era. Here, cedar-shingled, turreted mansions have been restored or reinvented as luxury B&Bs, including the **Normandy Inn** *(21 Tuttle Ave. 908-449-7172).* The long, noncommercial boardwalk makes for great biking, while Third Avenue abounds with shopping. History lovers enjoy the restored bog-iron workers' village at nearby **Allaire State Park** *(County Rd. 524, Farmingdale. 908-938-2371. Parking fee weekends).* Dating from the 1820s, it includes the furnace, the forge, shops, stores, houses, and the steam-powered **Pine Creek Railroad** *(908-938-5524. Late June–mid-Sept. daily, mid-Sept.–late June weekends; fare).*

South on N.J. 35 is **Island Beach State Park** ★ *(Seaside Park. 908-793-0506. Adm. fee),* 3,000 acres of barrier beach, dunes, and wetlands stretching about 10 miles south to **Barnegat Lighthouse.** Perched along the Atlantic flyway, the park lures birdwatchers, who flock here in spring and fall to spot warblers, Canada geese, and common terns. There's a bathing beach, but most of the park is reserved for beach walking, surf fishing, picnicking, and horseback riding.

Leaving the shore on N.J. 37, you penetrate the northern rim of New Jersey's Twilight Zone, the **Pine Barrens.** A century ago, this area thrived with iron-mining, glass-making, and cranberry-growing communities. Today, the region comprises the million-acre Pinelands National Reserve. ❽ **Double Trouble State Park** ★ *(Pinewald-Keswick Rd., off County Rd. 530. 908-341-6662)* offers a glimpse into the lives of "Pineys'" in a turn-of-the-century ghost town. Only partially restored, the town includes a sawmill, a school, a packing house, and pickers' cottages set around cranberry bogs. The park also offers hiking and canoeing.

Kirbys Mill, Medford

Zigzagging through the **Lebanon State Forest** *(609-726-1191)* section of the Pine Barrens, you pass through **Chatsworth,** site of the popular **Chatsworth Cranberry Festival** *(White Horse Inn, Main St. 609-859-9701. Parking fee)* the third weekend in October. Breaking out of the forest, you find yourself in a land of lakes surrounded by the cedar log cabins of the resort-turned-suburb of **Medford Lakes.**

Before returning to the world of interstate highways, you might want to stop in ❾ **Medford** to see **Kirbys Mill** *(275 Church Rd. 609-654-0768. Sun. in June-Aug.),* a restored 1778 gristmill. If you have a canoe, go for a paddle on the South Branch Rancocas, which powers the mill. Return to Trenton via N.J. 541, I-295, and I-195.

The Highlands

● **200 miles** ● **2 to 3 days** ● **Spring through autumn**

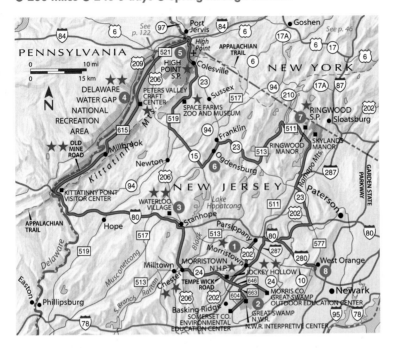

Exploring the hilly country west of New York City's Jersey suburbs—with its roadside fruit stands, antique and craft shows, and abundant farmland—is like rambling through a country fair. The trip begins on the edge of suburbia in Morristown, the site of the Continental Army's winter quarters and a panoply of historic houses, estates, and farms. You then head south to the boardwalk trails of the Great Swamp National Wildlife Refuge before swinging north to the country village of Chester. Nearby lies New Jersey's largest lake, Hopatcong, and a picture-perfect ghost town revived as a living history museum. Traveling through the Delaware River Valley—popular with hikers, campers, and canoeists—this rural drive brings you to the state's highest point. Arching back to the starting point, you stop to visit three historic mansions.

During the Revolutionary War, George Washington and his troops spent two winters at ❶ **Morristown**★ *(Historic Morris Visitors Center 201-631-5151)* to protect the town's powder and arms industry from the British. Divided into four units and covering nearly 1,700 acres, **Morristown National Historical Park**★ *(Information Center, 10 Washington Pl. 201-539-2085. Adm. fee)* commemorates those bitter cold winters in 1777 and 1779-80. Start with a visit to **Washington's Headquarters Unit** *(Next to Information Center. Adm. fee)*, which preserves the house that served as Washington's office. The adjacent **Historical Museum and Library** *(201-539-2085)* details the soldiers' hardships.

East of the historical park, the **Morris Museum** *(6 Normandy Heights Rd., off Columbia Rd. 201-538-0454. Adm. fee)* has exhibits on Native American and colonial life, fine arts and natural science. Nearby, the **George G. Frelinghuysen Arboretum** *(53 E. Hanover Ave. 201-326-7600. Donation)* is a 127-acre estate with an extensive collection of plants and trees, surrounding an 1891 colonial revival mansion.

144

Ford's Mansion, Morristown National Historical Park

Heading back into the center of town, stop by **Acorn Hall** *(68 Morris Ave. 201-267-3465. March-Dec. Thurs. and Sun.; adm. fee)*, an 1853 Italianate Victorian mansion; and the colonial **Schuyler-Hamilton House** *(5 Olyphant Pl. 201-267-4039. Tues. and Sun.; adm. fee)*, where Alexander Hamilton, Washington's aide-de-camp and the future secretary of the treasury, once lived.

Toward the north side of town stands **Historic Speedwell** *(333 Speedwell Ave. 201-540-0211. May-Oct. Thurs.-Sun.; adm. fee)*, a Georgian-style mansion that preserves the estate and factory of a self-made 19th-century iron baron. At nearby **Fosterfields Living Historical Farm** *(73 Kahdena Rd., off Madison Ave. 201-326-7645. April-Oct. Wed.-Sun.; adm. fee)*, watch interpreters tending the land, sheering sheep, and milking cows according to 19th-century tradition. You can also wander around the 18th-century Gothic Revival house where Paul Revere's grandson once lived.

Now head north on US 202 to **Parsippany** and 26-acre **Craftsman Farms** *(2352 N.J. 10. 201-540-1165. Grounds open year-round, museum April-Oct. Thurs. and Sat.-Sun.; adm. fee for museum)*, where Gustav Stickley, a leading figure in the arts and crafts movement, resided in the early 1900s. The designer's functional, clean-line "Mission" style furniture decorating the chestnut log house was a revolutionary change from the Victorian age's heavy, embellished style that preceded it.

The drive returns to Morristown, to two more Morristown National Historical Park sites. At **Fort Nonsense** (*Off Washington St.*), Washington allegedly kept his troops busy building a useless fortress—hence the name—during the early months of 1777. At **Jockey Hollow**★★ (*5 miles S of town on Jockey Hollow Rd., off US 202/Mt. Kemble Ave. and Tempe Wick Rd. 201-539-2085*), you will see the fields and forests where the Continental Army weathered relentless snowstorms during the winter of 1779-80. Conditions here were so trying that a mutiny broke out, but troops loyal to the Revolution prevailed. While there are five reconstructed soldiers huts and a farmhouse the generals used, the chief attraction to Jockey Hollow is the solitude, vistas of fields and forests, and 25 miles of hiking trails.

Next jog southeast on County Rds. 646, 663, and 604 to the ❷ **Great Swamp National Wildlife Refuge** (*Long Hill Rd. 201-425-1222. Visitor Center open Mon.-Fri.*). Eight miles of hiking trails—many on boardwalks—lead through oaks, sumacs, and duckweed to a marsh where great blue herons, redwing blackbirds, deer, foxes, wood frogs, and 40-pound snapping turtles move to seasonal rhythms. Bordering the swamp's east side, the **Morris County Great Swamp Outdoor Education Center** (*Southern Blvd. 201-635-6629*) has two short trails over woods, fields, marshes, and swamps. On the swamp's western edge, the **Somerset County Environmental Education Center** (*Lord Stirling Rd. 908-766-2489*) boasts a museum, 8.5 miles of hiking trails, and an environmental library.

The country drive backtracks to Jockey Hollow and proceeds west on N.J. 24 through rolling woodlands and across streams to the village of **Chester**★★. A former stagecoach stop and iron ore boomtown, Chester hibernated through much of this century until awakening in the 1970s to find itself just the kind of country village daytrippers from New York City and the suburbs sought to escape from hectic lives. Dozens of antique dealers, galleries, and specialty shops charm shoppers—and because of the competition, you really can get some good buys here. **Cooper Mill** (*1 mile W of town, on N.J. 24. 908-879-5463. July-Aug. Fri.-Tues., spring and fall weekends*) offers tours of a restored 1826 gristmill on the Black River. An 1810 inn, the **Publick House** (*111 Main St. 908-879-6878*) figures as a popular spot for lunch, dinner, or overnight stays.

Head a few miles north on US 206 to the village of **Stanhope,** which commands a strategic site near Lake

The Highlands

Waterloo Village, near Stanhope

Bear Facts

It's hard to believe that a person in post-industrial America would associate bears with New Jersey. But far-ranging black bears find the hundreds of square miles of public forest in the Delaware Water Gap region attractive habitat. In fact, over the last couple of years, bears have invaded campsites nearly every night at High Point State Park. Normally furtive, the bears lack all self-control when it comes to food, and they possess noses that can scent grub from long distances away. Picnickers in the area should keep food in sealed containers, stored in a vehicle, or risk a close encounter with a feisty ursine.

Hopatcong—New Jersey's largest freshwater body. Perched on the hilly, wooded banks of the Musconetcong River and the defunct Morris Canal, historic ❸ **Waterloo Village**★★ *(Waterloo Rd. 201-347-0900. Mid-April–mid Dec. Wed.-Sun.; adm. fee)* contains over 28 prosperous houses, businesses, and public structures that survive from the hamlet's boom days as a Revolutionary War-era iron forge and 19th-century transportation center. Stroll among costumed guides and artisans, and visit the restored period houses and a re-created Minisink Indian village. From May to October the **Waterloo Festival of the Arts** *(201-347-0900)* draws crowds for concerts, antique and craft shows, dances, and Oktoberfest.

Farmstands and pick-your-own operations dot the roadside as you head west on I-80. One of the best known stops for country lovers is 392-acre **Matarazzo Farms**★ *(5 miles S of Hope, on Cty. Rd. 519. 908-475-3872. April–late Dec.),* where you can pick everything in season from beans and peppers to gladiolas and strawberries, buy fresh baked goods, and sample wine at **Four Sisters Winery** *(908-475-3671).*

Driving farther west, you soon spy a great cleft cut through Kittatinny Ridge—the **Delaware Water Gap.** Flanking a 40-mile stretch of the Delaware River, which was responsible for carving the gap, the ❹ **Delaware Water Gap National Recreation Area**★★ is a 70,000-acre wilderness prime for hiking, canoeing, camping, and fishing. Stop by the **Kittatinny Point Visitor Center** *(Off I-80 near toll bridge, before river. 908-496-4458. April-Oct. daily, Nov.-March weekends)* for information and maps. Then head north on the river's east bank, along unspoiled **Old Mine Road**★★. A short way down the road, stretch your legs along the **Copper Mine Trail**★, a 1.5-mile walk past old mines to the top of Kittatinny Ridge, with a fine overlook of the gap. The road more or less parallels the **Appalachian Trail;** you can pick it up at Kittatinny Point and hike along the ridge.

About 12 miles north of the Visitor Center stands **Millbrook Village** *(Old Mine Rd. 908-841-9531. Mid-June–mid-Oct. daily, May–mid June weekends),* a living history reconstruction of a 19th-century Delaware River Valley town featuring costumed interpreters. Farther north, you discover **Peters Valley Craft Center**★ *(County Rd. 615. 201-948-5200. June-Aug. Fri.-Sun.)*. Summer workshops draw blacksmiths, woodworkers, fabricmakers, weavers, potters, and jewelers, whose studios are housed in historic buildings.

Following Old Mine Road, County Rd. 521, and US 6 to N.J. 23 south brings you to the crest of the Kittatinny Mountains—the state's highest point (1,803 feet)—and ❺ **High Point State Park**★ *(N.J. 23. 201-875-4800)*. A popular retreat for picnicking, swimming, boating, fishing, hiking, and camping, the 14,056-acre park spreads south for 8 miles. At the park's northern end, a scenic drive winds to the mountain summit, where a 220-foot observation monument offers sweeping vistas of the Poconos and Catskills.

Heading south on N.J. 23 and County Rd. 519, the drive soon reaches a classic example of a vanished institution—the family-run roadside zoo. Prospering since 1927, 100-acre **Space Farms Zoo and Museum**★ *(Cty. Rd. 519, W of Sussex. 201-875-5800. May-Oct.; adm. fee)* features over 500 animals in natural settings. The farm claims to be the world's largest private collection of North American wildlife, and you will believe it when you see the menagerie of grizzly bears, lions, deer, wolves—more than 100 species in all. In addition, a museum displays 100,000 antiques ranging from arrowheads to old clocks.

From the zoo, continue south on County Rd. 519, then southeast on N.J. 15, then north on County Rd. 517 through rolling farmland to the town of ❻ **Ogdensburg** and the **Sterling Hill Mining Museum**★ *(30 Plant St., off Brooks Flat Rd. 201-209-7212. Tours April-Nov. daily, March and Dec. weekends; adm. fee)*. Preserving one of the state's

High Point State Park, near Colesville

Formal gardens at Ringwood Manor, Ringwood State Park

richest zinc mines, along with antique mining equipment, Sterling Hill is the place to learn the region's mining story. Rock hounds prospect around the old dump mines. If you don't want to do the hunting yourself, visit the displays at the **Franklin Mineral Museum and Mine Replica** (*Evans St. 201-827-3481. April-Nov. daily, March weekends; adm. fee*), in nearby **Franklin.**

Now take N.J. 23 east to County Rds. 513 and 511, which carry you into the wooded Ramapo Mountains to **❼ Ringwood State Park**★ (*201-962-7031*). While the park offers its share of hiking, boating, fishing, bathing, and picnicking, the real attractions here are two historic mansions: **Ringwood Manor** (*201-962-7031. Wed.-Sun.; adm. fee Sat.-Sun.*) was the 78-room home of the Hewitt family, who ruled the area's iron-mining industry for nearly a century; and the 44-room Jacobean **Skylands Manor** (*201-962-9534. First Sun. every month; adm. fee*)—a stockbroker's 1920s extravagance—is surrounded by the 96-acre **New Jersey State Botanical Gardens** (*201-962-7527. Adm. fee June-Aug.*).

Edison's paraphernalia, Edison National Historic Site, West Orange

To cap this drive, follow County Rd. 511 and N.J. 23 south, I-80 west, and I-280 east to **❽ West Orange** and the **Edison National Historic Site**★★ (*Main St. and Lakeside Ave. 201-736-0550. Tours Wed.-Sun.; adm. fee.*). Commemorating the great inventor, the site preserves the lab where Thomas Edison worked from 1886 to 1931. Among several rooms you'll visit is a reproduction of the world's first movie studio. At the historic site, buy tickets and make reservations for a tour of nearby **Glenmont** (*201-736-0550. Wed.-Sun.; adm. fee*), the 23-room Queen Anne mansion where Edison and his wife, Minna, lived. Articles of clothing hang in the restored rooms, leaving you with the feeling that the Edisons have just stepped out.

Return to Morristown via I-280, I-80, and I-287.

Jersey Shore Loop

● **210 miles** ● **3 to 4 days** ● **Late spring to early fall**

To circle the New Jersey shore is to revisit simpler times. This trip begins on the bustling boardwalk of Atlantic City, and then travels south through a string of beach towns, each with its own distinct character. At the state's southern tip, the gingerbread architecture of Cape May revives the Victorian era. Salt marshes are a strong presence as the route curls around New Jersey's southern tip and into the villages of Delaware Bay, where oyster schooners and colonial houses endure. You will see how glass becomes art at Wheaton Village before this drive carries you to the sprawling Pine Barrens, home to the legendary Jersey Devil.

With more than 37 million visitors a year, ❶ **Atlantic City**★ *(Convention and Visitor Authority 609-449-7130 or 888-228-4748)* is the hands-down favorite mid-Atlantic resort for travelers for whom gambling, crowds, glitzy shows, and sea breezes equal fun. The town claims to have the world's first boardwalk, built in 1870 to keep sand out of the hotels, and the young at heart have seen those boards as a path to a carefree world ever since. Today the boardwalk stretches 4.5 miles—a freeway for walkers, joggers, bikers,

Jersey Shore Loop

Atlantic City beachfront

and riders in the famous rolling chairs *(609-347-7148. Fare)*.

Since the legalization of gambling here in 1977, twelve casinos and a new convention center have replaced the original, lavish, turn-of-the-century structures. But the 5.8-billion-dollar renaissance may well be eclipsed by the 7 billion dollars in new investments due by the year 2000. Six new casinos and new transportation facilities will add to the city's identification with its board-game counterpart, Monopoly. While you can gamble here 24 hours a day, people-watching and window shopping are simple pleasures for many visitors who come for a morning, park in a casino lot near the beach, cruise the boardwalk, buy some saltwater taffy, and explore the more than one hundred establishments along the pier at **The Shops at Ocean One** *(Boardwalk and Arkansas Ave. 609-347-8082)*. You can also check out the **Trump Taj Mahal Casino Resort** *(1000 Boardwalk at Virginia Ave. 609-449-1000 or 800-825-8786)*, which almost lives up to its namesake in opulence and—some say—excess. The **Steel Pier,** built in 1898, stretches out in front. And if you're here in September, you may be treated to a bevy of beauties during the Miss America Pageant week *(609-347-7571 for schedule)*.

To get a feel for the city's pre-gambling days, stop in at the **Atlantic City Historical Museum** *(Boardwalk and New Jersey Ave. 609-347-5839)*, on the restored Garden Pier. Nearby, the exhibits at the **Ripley's "Believe It Or Not!"**® **Museum** *(Boardwalk and New York Ave. 609-347-2001. Adm. fee)* are sure to intrigue the whole family. To escape the crowds and skyscrapers, wander over to **Gardiner's Basin Maritime Park** *(Bounded by the bay and New Hampshire, Rhode Island, and Parkside Aves.)*, a good place to sit and check out the yachts.

Say goodbye to Atlantic City and head south on Atlantic Avenue. As you pass through the town of **Margate City,** give a wave to **Lucy the Margate Elephant** *(Decatur and Atlantic Aves. 609-823-6473. May-Oct.; adm. fee),* a 65-foot "folly" built in 1881 to attract tourists. Refurbished and open to the public for tours, she still does the job.

Cross the Ocean City-Longport Bridge *(toll)* and head south on Ocean Drive—marked with seagull signs—for your first view of the bays, salt marshes, and grassy islands that lie west of the beach resorts. Myriad inlets along the drive to Cape May offer uncrowded sites for fishing, bird-watching, and picnicking. But beware: Ocean Drive passes through thickly settled resorts where traffic lights make for frustrating travel after 10 a.m. every day of the summer.

Farther down the shore, ❷ **Ocean City** *(Chamber of Commerce 609-399-2629 or 800-232-2465)* is a onetime Christian summer retreat where an eclectic mix of middle-class summer houses on tiny lots has nearly filled the 8-mile-long island. Families love the broad beaches, 2.5 miles of boardwalk, and summer concerts at the **Music Pier.**

The **Ocean City Historical Museum** *(1735 Simpson Ave. 609-399-1801. May-Oct. Mon.-Sat., Nov.-April Tues.-Sat.)* illustrates town history with an array of period rooms and displays, including one on the *Cindia,* wrecked off these shores in 1901. The museum also administers a second site, a **seashore cottage** *(1139 Wesley Ave. Adm. fee)* depicting the style of a summer home from the 1920s to the 1940s.

The town's south end offers dunes and empty beaches under the protection of **Corson's Inlet State Park** *(Ocean Dr. and 59th St. 609-861-2404),* the best place on the southern Jersey Shore to see barrier islands in their wild state. Sometimes you can spot humpback whales breaching just offshore.

Farther south, **Strathmere** and **Sea Isle City** *(Tourist Information 609-263-8687)* look like scaled-down versions of Ocean City. But zoning ordinances and fewer houses seem to equal less traffic in spite of the fishing fleets docked here and in the towns south of Townsends Inlet.

Crossing the inlet bridge to **Avalon** *(Chamber of Commerce 609-967-3936)* and **Stone Harbor** *(Chamber of Commerce 609-368-6101),* you'll notice bigger houses and yards that proclaim this is upper-middle-class turf. You need to buy a beach permit to get waterside, but it's worth it: Avalon's dunes, one of the highest dune areas in the state,

---

Jersey Tea Party

Nearly a year after the Boston Tea Party and subsequent British blockade of Boston Harbor, New Jersey patriots protested English tyranny in December 1774 by disguising themselves in warpaint and burning the cargo of tea from the British brig *Greyhound.* Not much has changed since then at the port town of **Greenwich** on the Cohansey River, where the protest site is marked by the **Tea Burner's Monument.** Colonial and federal architecture dominates Ye Greate Street, and farmers, watermen, and gentry keep to their independent lifestyle. A visit to the 1730 **Gibbon House Museum** *(Ye Greate Street. 609-455-4055. April-Nov. Tues.-Sun.; donation)* will expand your knowledge of the town's Quaker history.

151

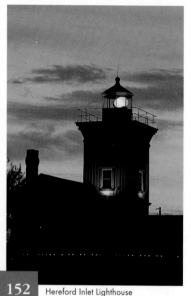

Hereford Inlet Lighthouse

surround you with nature—not traffic, concrete, or arcades. In addition to an upscale village center, **Stone Harbor** offers the **Stone Harbor Bird Sanctuary** *(Third Ave., 111th-116th Sts. 609-368-5102)*, a nesting ground for egrets, herons, and ibises.

The three towns that make up the island known as the **Wildwoods** *(Visitor Center 609-729-9000 or 800-992-9732)* are a different story. With six-story hotels and condos, miles of commercial boardwalk, and five amusement parks, the Wildwoods rival Atlantic City for development. However, its 5 miles of beaches are free and safe for swimming, since the surf line is almost a thousand feet offshore. By night the Wildwoods vibrate to flashing neon, calliope music, and the spin of game wheels. You either love it or hate it.

But there are other attractions. At the **Hereford Inlet Lighthouse** *(1st and Central Aves., N. Wildwood. 609-522-4520. April-Nov.)*, the tower's Gothic Victorian architecture and cottage gardens recall the days when the Swedish fishing village of Anglesea was the only sign of human life here (it's since been incorporated into North Wildwood). Take a ride on the bay aboard the Cape Dinner Cruises *(6006 Park Blvd., Wildwood Crest. 609-523-8989 or 800-942-5373. April-Oct.; fare. Reservations required)*.

But the greatest escape of all sits across the causeway at ❸ **Cape May★★.** With towering trees, gaslit streets, and 600 restored Victorian buildings, the entire town is a National Historic Landmark. One of the oldest seaside resorts in America, Cape May hosted its first vacationers in the 1760s. But when a great fire in 1878 destroyed the town, residents rebuilt in gingerbread. Neighboring resorts with more amusements eventually eclipsed Cape May, and the town settled into dormancy until the 1970s, when it awoke to find itself a treasure of Victorian architecture.

Today, Cape May sparkles. Start your visit with a stop at the "onion dome," **Cape May's Welcome Center** *(405 Lafayette St. 609-884-9562 or 800-227-2297)*, in a former church. Here you can pick up maps, brochures, and advice to guide you around the town's asymmetrical street plan or direct you to a trolley, carriage, gaslit, or ghost tour. Also helpful, the **Mid-Atlantic Center for the Arts** *(609-884-2787)* sponsors a number of local tours. The center is located within the 18-room **Emlen Physick Estate** *(1048 Washington St. 609-884-5404)*, an 1879 Victorian house-museum displaying original furnishings.

Closed to traffic, the **Washington Street Mall** *(Bet.*

Ocean and Perry Sts.) harbors specialty shops, restaurants, and cafés. More than 50 B&Bs try to outdo each other with period decor and hearty breakfasts. Even monumental structures once considered too large to be restored are being renewed, such as the luxurious **Southern Mansion** *(720 Washington St. 609-884-7171)* and **Congress Hall** *(251 Beach Ave. 609-884-8421),* a hotel that hosted Presidents Buchanan, Pierce, Grant, and Harrison.

Cape May appeals to quiet travelers. Morning beach walks searching for "Cape May diamonds," globs of silica polished by the surf, can grow addicting. Birders head to **Cape May Migratory Bird Refuge** *(Sunset Blvd. 856-785-1735)* and adjacent **Cape May Point State Park**★★ *(End of Lighthouse Ave. 609-884-2159)* to watch waterfowl, plus walk the trails and explore the dunes. End your day at the state park's **Cape May Point Lighthouse** *(609-884-8656. Closed Mon.-Fri. Dec.-Feb.; adm. fee),* with its vista of Atlantic shoals.

Follow US 9 to **Historic Cold Spring Village** *(4 miles N of Cape May, at 720 US 9. 609-898-2300. Daily mid-June–Aug., weekends early June and Sept.; adm. fee),* where a community of crafts people inhabit more than 20 restored buildings, re-creating rural life in the 1800s. A few miles north in the midst of a 6,000-acre salt marsh, the **Wetlands Institute** *(1075 Stone Harbor Blvd. 609-368-1211. Closed Sun.-Mon. Oct.-May; adm. fee),* is a good place for birdwatching from its observation tower and wetland trails.

You will find Edens of a different sort at the **Cape May County Park and Zoo** *(707 US 9, Cape May Courthouse. 609-465-5271),* with re-created natural habitats including an African savannah, and nature and bike trails. For a better understanding of 18th-century life in the region, stop in at the **Cape May County Historical Museum** *(504 US 9, Cape May Courthouse. 609-465-3535. Mid-April–mid-Nov. Tues.-Sat., Sat. only rest of year; adm. fee).* Or wander the 30-acres of **Leaming's Run Gardens**★ *(1845 US 9N, Swainton. 609-465-5871. Mid-May–mid-Oct.; adm. fee),* a colonial farm with 25 theme gardens, considered some of the best in the mid-Atlantic.

Admiring an osprey at Wetlands Institute

From here follow N.J. 83 and N.J. 47 northwest into the Delaware Bay area, where marshes, tidal creeks, and sparkling water compose the scenery once you get off the main route. One of the region's classic views comes from wandering the 18th-century village of ❹ **Mauricetown** and looking down the Maurice River. From here, follow County Rds. 649 and 553 to the rough-and-ready settlements of **Port Norris, Shellpile,** and **Bivalve**★ and observe the watermen who fish for oysters and crabs as their ancestors have for centuries. Bivalve is the home of the **Delaware Bay Schooner Project**★ *(2800 High St., Bivalve. 856-785-2060. Adm. fee),* whose restored oyster schooner carries passengers on educational sails into the bay.

Continuing on County Rd. 553, you'll come to **Bridgeton.** With 2,200 buildings from the colonial, federal, and Victorian periods, the tidewater port is New Jersey's largest historic district. But Bridgeton remains a working town. Pick up walking tour maps and directions to local museums at the **Tourist Information Center** *(50 E. Broad St. 856-451-4551 or 800-319-3379),* a restored railway depot.

Go east to ❺ **Millville** and **Wheaton Village** *(1501 Glasstown Rd. 856-825-6800 or 800-998-4552. Closed Mon.-Tues. Jan.-March; adm. fee),* a crafts village designed around a glassmaking theme, with artist demonstrations and displays at the **Museum of American Glass.**

Then head northeast to Hammonton. Once County Rd. 542 leaves town, the persistent evergreens signal your entrance into the **Pine Barrens** *(Visitor Information 609-894-9342).* Some one million acres of pine forest are protected in this regional preserve. Within it lies ❻ **Batsto Village**★★ *(Off County Rd. 542. 609-561-0024. Summer parking fee),* a 19th-century settlement restored to its former days as a bog iron and glassmaking center. The sights here include a sawmill, worker's houses, and the country estate of Philadelphia financier Joseph Wharton. The **Wharton State Forest**

Cape May's Victoriana

office *(County Rd. 542. 609-561-0024)*, also in the preserve, provides information about the extensive hiking, canoeing, and camping opportunities in the state forest.

Following N.J. 563, then Alt. N.J. 561 to the pines' eastern edge, you will discover the **Renault Winery** *(72 N. Bremen Ave., Galloway Township. 609-965-2111. Adm. fee)*, offering tastings, tours, and a glass museum. **Smithville** *(Alt. N.J. 561. 609-652-7777)* is a restored village of more than 30 houses, shops, and restaurants built around an inn dating from 1787. In ❼ **Oceanville,** stop at the **Noyes Museum of Art** *(Lily Lake Rd. 609-652-8848. Wed.-Sun.; adm. fee)* to take in the collection of fine and regional folk arts. From the central gallery, look across the lake toward the 42,000-acre **Edwin B. Forsythe National Wildlife Refuge** *(Great Creek Rd. 609-652-1665. Adm. fee)*. When overwintering snow geese arrive in October, everyone stops and watches. To return to Atlantic City, take US 9 south.

NEW YORK

New York State Division of Tourism
General information *800-CALL-NYS.*

Division of Fish and Wildlife Hunting
and fishing license information *717-457-
3521.*

**New York State Department of Parks,
Recreation and Historic Preservation**
General information for all areas of New
York except the Adirondacks and Catskills
Forest Preserves *518-474-0456.* Camp-
ground reservations *800-456-CAMP.*

**New York State Department of Environ-
mental Conservation** Campground
information for Adirondacks and Catskills
Forest Preserves *518-457-7433.*

New York State Thruway Authority
Road conditions *800-847-8929.*

PENNSYLVANIA

Pennsylvania Department of Tourism
General information *717-787-5453.*

Bureau of State Parks State parks and
campground information *800-63-PARKS.*

Fish and Boat Commission Fishing
license and boating information *717-657-
4518.*

Game Commission Hunting information
717-783-4250.

Department of Transportation Road
and weather conditions *888-783-6783.*

Pennsylvania Travel Council B&B listings *717-783-5186.*

NEW JERSEY

**New Jersey Division of Travel and
Tourism** General information *609-292-
2470.*

Division of Fish, Game and Wildlife
Hunting and fishing license information
609-292-2965.

Division of Parks and Forestry State
parks and campground information *609-
984-0370.*

State Police Road conditions *609-882-
2000.*

**Bed & Breakfast Innkeepers Associa-
tion of New Jersey** B&B listings *732-
449-3535.*

HOTEL & MOTEL CHAINS
**(Accommodations in all three states
unless otherwise noted)**
Best Western International *800-528-1234*
Budget Host *800-BUD HOST* (except N.J.)
Choice Hotels *800-4-CHOICE*
Clarion Hotels *800-CLARION*
Comfort Inns *800-228-5150*
Courtyard by Marriott *800-321-2211*
Days Inn *800-325-2525*
Doubletree Hotels and Guest Suites
800-222-TREE
Econo Lodge *800-446-6900*

Embassy Suites *800-362-2779*
Four Seasons Hotels and Resorts *800-426-
0333* (except N.J.)
Hampton Inn *800-HAMPTON*
Hilton Hotels *800-HILTONS*
Holiday Inns *800-HOLIDAY*
Howard Johnson *800-654-2000*
Hyatt Hotels and Resorts *800-233-1234*
Marriott Hotels Resorts Suites *800-228-9290*
Motel Six *800-466-8356*
Quality Inns-Hotels-Suites *800-228-5151*
Radisson Hotels Intl. *800-333-3333*
Ramada Inns *800-2-RAMADA*
Red Roof Inns *800-843-7663*
Ritz-Carlton *800-241-3333* (except N.J.)
ITT Sheraton Hotels & Inns *800-325-3535*
Super 8 Motels *800-843-1991*
Travelodge International, Inc. *800-255-3050*
Utell International *800-223-9868*
Westin Hotels and Resorts *800-228-3000*
(except N.J.)

ILLUSTRATIONS CREDITS

Photographs in this book are by Pete Souza,
except the following: 8 Michael Melford;
12 (upper) Joe McNally/Sygma; 18 Steve
McCurry; 21 Jake Rajs; 22 Steve McCurry; 27
Joe McNally; 34 Ted Spiegel; 52 (lower)
Bob Krist; 107 (lower) Fallingwater/The
Western Pennsylvania Conservancy; 130
Bill Ballenberg; 141 Michael Melford.

NOTES ON AUTHOR
AND PHOTOGRAPHER

RANDALL PEFFER is a widely published travel
writer who has written about Delaware
Bay, Massachusetts' North Shore, Catalonia,
Bermuda, and Boston for NATIONAL GEO-
GRAPHIC magazine and NATIONAL GEOGRAPHIC
TRAVELER. He teaches literature and writing
at Phillips Academy in Andover, Massachusetts. His narrative *Waterman,* about the
lives of the Chesapeake's fishermen, was
the Baltimore *Sun's* "Critics Choice."

A native of South Dartmouth, Massachusetts, freelance photographer PETE SOUZA
has lived in Arlington, Virginia, for the
past 13 years. A frequent contributor to
the National Geographic Society, he has
photographed two articles for NATIONAL
GEOGRAPHIC magazine and half of
*National Geographic's Driving Guide to
America—Washington, D.C., and Envi-
rons.* Souza has won numerous photo-
journalism awards, including a first and
second place in the prestigious Pictures
of the Year competition for his coverage
of the Million Man March in Washington, D.C.

Index

159

160

Composition for this book by the National
Geographic Society Book Division. Printed
and bound by R.R. Donnelly & Sons, Willard,
Ohio. Color separations by Digital Color
Image, Pensauken, New Jersey. Paper by
Consolidated/Alling & Cory, Willow Grove,
Pennsylvania. Cover printed by Miken Com-
panies, Inc. Cheektowaga, New York.

LIBRARY OF CONGRESS CATALOGING-IN-PUBLICATION DATA

Peffer, Randall S.
    New York and Pennsylvania and New Jersey / by Randy Peffer ;
  photographed by Pete Souza ; prepared by the Book Division,
  National Geographic Society, Washington, D.C.
        p. cm. — (National Geographic's driving guides to America)
    Includes index.
    ISBN 0-7922-3431-6
    1. New York (State)—Tours. 2. Pennsylvania—Tours. 3. New
Jersey—Tours. 4. Automobile travel—New York (State)—Guidebooks.
5. Automobile travel—Pennsylvania—Guidebooks. 6. Automobile
travel—New Jersey—Guidebooks.   I. Souza, Pete.
II. National Geographic Society (U.S.).   Book Division. III. Title.
IV. Series.
F117.3.P44 1997
917.4—dc21   97-22435
                                                             CIP

Visit the Society's Web site at www.nationalgeographic.com